# THE HALF-PINT GUIDE TO CRAFT BREWERIES

## NORTHERN CALIFORNIA

**Deirdre Greene and Nigel Quinney**

Roaring Forties Press
1053 Santa Fe Avenue
Berkeley, CA 94706
www.roaringfortiespress.com

Cover design by Kim Rusch; interior design by Nigel Quinney.

ISBN 978-1-938901-71-3 (print)
ISBN 978-1-938901-72-0 (ebook)

# Contents

INTRODUCTION IV

ABBREVIATIONS VIII


NORTH COAST **2**

THE NORTH AND EAST **12**

ON (AND OFF) I-80 **28**

WINE COUNTRY **50**

EAST BAY **64**

SAN FRANCISCO AND MARIN **90**

SOUTH BAY AND SANTA CRUZ **118**


ALPHABETICAL LIST OF BREWERIES **142**

CHEERS **144**

# Introduction

Welcome to *The Half-Pint Guide!*

(That's pretty much it! We just wanted to say hello and welcome. If you want to skip the rest of this introduction, please go right ahead and do so. This is, after all, only a book. You've seen books before. You know how they work. No batteries, instructions, ID, or shirt and shoes required. This little book is full of some of the best craft breweries in Northern California, and if you want to know what their founders and brewers think about them, just dive right in. But if you're one of those people who like to know what they're getting themselves into, then, please, let us bend your ear for a couple of minutes.)

We wrote this book for people like us. People who enjoy chatting with a brewer across a bar about favorite beers, biggest achievements, and funniest stories. People who have stumbled on a fabulous brewery that they had no idea even existed. People who—scary thought!— have found themselves in an unfamiliar corner of California and real-ized, "OMG, I do not know where the nearest craft brewery is. Help!"

So, we thought we'd put together a guide that does three things.

One of those things is to cover great breweries in lots of different parts of the state, not just in the hoppy hot spots. The idea is that if you're from the mountains visiting the beach, or from the beach visit-ing the desert, or from . . . well, you get the idea, this book will help you find a fine place to wet your whistle.

The second thing is not only to provide nuts-and-bolts information about each brewery—important but basic stuff like where it is and when it's open—but also to dig deeper and uncover a brewery's story and personality. What makes it tick, what makes its founders proud, what do its regulars like best about it?

And the third thing is to let the breweries tell that story them-selves, in their own words. As you'll see once you stop reading this introduction (if you haven't already!) and start dipping into the rest of the book, we asked each brewery more or less the same questions. The answers, though, are often wildly different—as different and as wild as the brewers and the breweries themselves.

A lot of books about beer are written by people who know a lot about beer and have a lot of opinions about breweries. And that is cool. But it's also sometimes a bit boring, because professional beer drinkers (now, there's a job!) and full-time critics can get a little jaded and carry around some big biases. One of the best things about visiting California's craft breweries is that wherever you go, you meet friendly brewers full of energy, enthusiasm, and passion for what they're doing—and for what their fellow brewers are doing on the next block or in the next town. This book is filled with that spirit. It's also filled with the kind of information and stories that only a brewer or an owner can tell you about his or her beer and brewery.

You might think that all that information and all those stories would easily fill a 1,000-barrel fermenter. Yet, here they are in a book called *The Half-Pint Guide*—a name inspired in large part by its small size. Why didn't we produce a book the size of the Beijing telephone directory?

The simple answer is that we wanted to end up with a book small enough to keep in your car's glove compartment or to fit in the back pocket of your jeans. (Try it! It really does fit in your back pocket— unless you're very petite or unless you're not so very petite but are wearing very petite jeans.) Keeping it half-pint sized also meant that we had to be selective, not comprehensive, in our coverage. So, we aimed to showcase just over 70 breweries, spread out across the region, each one of them fabulous, innovative, or individual in its own way. Some well-known breweries are not included, and some are; some of the breweries in here have been around since before the craft beer revolution started, and some are new additions to the dynamically changing, still-expanding craft beer landscape.

As you already know, craft brewing in California is a certifiable phenomenon. From small beginnings thirty years ago, it has blossomed—no, not blossomed, it's exploded—into a force of nature, a volcano of creativity, a tsunami of flavors washing over a land where beer drinkers once had few (and, let's be honest, pretty boring) choices. A few years ago, you'd walk into a bar and be faced with the same question: "Bud or Miller?" Today, you walk into a craft brewery and have an alphabet of options: an altbier or an amber, a blonde or a brown, a chocolate stout or a cream ale . . . all the way through to wits, wild ales, and winter warmers.

And what and who do we have to thank for this amazing choice? Small-scale businesses created and run by people who prize individuality and inventiveness, who love the beers they brew, who relish the chance to experiment with new beers, and who want to give other people the chance to love them. (Oh, and we should also thank ourselves, we who love that chance. If it wasn't for our heroic, selfless readiness to drink an always wonderful, often wild, and sometimes downright weird assortment of delicious beers, where would those craft brewers be? Just saying . . .)

We mention this because (A) it's true, and (B) it helped us define what we mean by a "craft brewery." A craft brewery, in our eyes, is a brewery owned by itself, not by a big, faceless corporation that owns lots and lots of things, that is in business purely for the money, and that measures its pleasure in IPOs and LBOs, not in ABVs and IBUs. We know that some craft breweries are owned in part by other craft breweries, and we're OK with that. But if a small brewery is owned by big business, you're not likely to find it in this book—simply because, if big business continues to snaffle up small breweries, creativity and diversity will give way to conformity and profitability, and we'll all be back to the old days of "Bud or Miller?" (Not that there's anything wrong with those two fine pilsners, but who wants a beer alphabet with just two letters?)

Ok, we've taken enough of your time. Please go and explore the rest of the book, which we hope you'll find not only a handy guide but also an interesting and sometimes eye-opening read. But before you head off, let us just mention a few housekeeping matters:

• The opening hours (like the street addresses and phone numbers) were accurate when we did the research for this book, but please check on a brewery's website before you head out in case those hours have recently changed.

• We've arranged the book into seven different geographic regions of Northern California: the North Coast (Mendocino up to the Oregon border); the North and East (separated by a range of mountains and lots of land, and probably two different trips); the Wine Country (Napa and Sonoma counties); On (and Off) I-80 (from the East Bay to Tahoe); San Francisco and Marin; the East Bay; and the South

Bay and Santa Cruz. The map on page 1 shows how we've divided up Northern California. A few breweries have locations in more than one region. In this book, however, we do not feature the same brewery in more than one region.

• There's a list of abbreviations on the next page. So, if you're not sure what "ABV" or "IBU" stands for, take a look.

• There's an index near the end of the book listing all the breweries that are included in the book alphabetically, so if you want to know at a glance which breweries are here and on what page, take a quick look at that.

• Right at the end of the book are some blank pages for you to jot down notes about the breweries you visit—or, if you prefer, you could use them to doodle pictures or play tic-tac-toe (a game invented, it's believed, by the ancient Egyptians, who really loved their beer).

• Please don't drink and drive. What are friends (or taxis) for?

Ok, we're done—there's nothing more to see here. But there's a state full of great beer to explore. And *The Half-Pint Guide* would love to tag along. ❊

# Abbreviations

ABV: alcohol by volume—a measurement of how much alcohol is in a given volume of a beverage. The higher the ABV percentage, the stronger the beer.

BBL: barrels—the standard size for a barrel in the United States is 31 gallons. Brewhouses are classified by the siuze they produce. Many craft breweries brew in 7- or 10-barrel batches.

GABF: Great American Beer Festival—a huge and prestigious beer event that takes place in Denver every year.

IBU: International Bitterness Units—a measurement of how bitter a beer is. The higher the IBU number, the more bitter the beer.

# Northern California

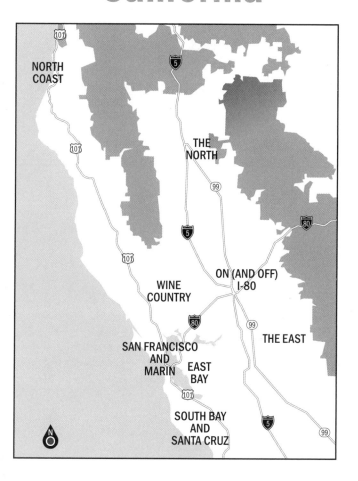

# North Coast

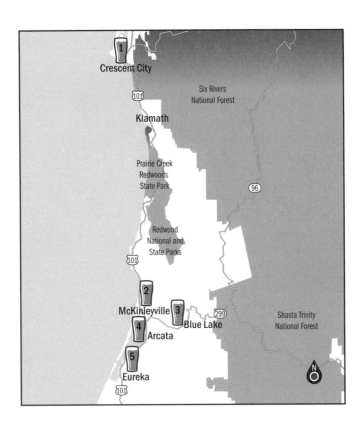

1. Port O'Pints Brewing Co., **Crescent City**
2. Six Rivers Brewery, **McKinleyville**
3. Mad River Brewing Co., **Blue Lake**
4. Redwood Curtain Brewing Co., **Arcata**
5. Lost Coast Brewery, **Eureka**

# PORT O'PINTS BREWING CO.

1215 Northcrest Dr., Crescent City, CA 95531
707-460-1154 • portopints.com

Mon.–Thurs. noon–9:30 pm; Fri. noon–midnight;
Sat. noon–midnight; Sun. noon–9 pm

**WHEN DID YOU OPEN?**

November 2015.

**WHAT ARE YOUR MOST POPULAR BEERS?**

Agate Ale, Del Norter Porter, Rumiano Milk Stout, Java Hut Coffee Stout, Bravo IPA, Warrior IPA.

**WHICH BEERS ARE YOU PROUDEST OF?**

The Del Norter Porter—it's always well received, and I have been brewing it since the beginning of my homebrewing days.

**HAVE ANY OF YOUR BEERS WON AWARDS?**

I have many awards as a homebrewer, none so far as a commercial brewer, but I have just started entering competitions in the past year.

**WHAT ARE THE BIGGEST CHALLENGES YOUR BREWERY HAS FACED?**

Getting through the TTB licensing and permitting process as they were getting their new system on board. Working through local and state guidelines in an area where there were no craft breweries open.

**WHAT'S THE ATMOSPHERE LIKE?**

We have a coastal/Celtic theme—an Irish pub with a

A Veteran Owned Business

maritime feel. The brewdeck is a pirate ship. We are self-proclaimed to have the only beer brewed in a pirate ship!

When our customers come into the pub, they often say, "I can't believe we are in Crescent City!" Many of our customers call our place cozy, comfortable, and a place where friends are made. Customers say, "It feels like this place has been here forever," but we've only been open for a couple of years!

## ARE YOU DOG & FAMILY FRIENDLY?

We are family friendly. Service dogs are permitted, but because we serve food, we ask other dogs to be tied outside or left in vehicles.

## DO YOU HAVE FOOD?

We have a small menu: Reuben panini; grilled cheese panini; bacon, lettuce, tomato, and avocado sandwich; Irish nachos; corned beef; Caesar salad; and soft pretzels with house-made beer cheese sauce or house-made honey mustard dip.

## WHAT ELSE CAN YOU TELL US?

We have an official greeter: our mannequin, Karma. Patrons love to dress her up and involve her in photo ops. We warn people to behave with her, as everyone knows that "Karma is a bitch!"

We host a Mr. Krampus party yearly for the release of our Mr. Krampus Holiday Ale. The entire town dresses up in their best "naughty" holiday attire to come celebrate the start of the Christmas season.

We host local and out-of-town music acts weekly and give away a free half yard of beer on your birthday! ❁

# SIX RIVERS BREWERY

1300 Central Ave., McKinleyville, CA 95519
707-839-7580 • sixriversbrewery.com

Mon. 4–11:30 pm; Tues. & Wed. 11:30 am–11:30 pm;
Thurs.–Sat. 11:30 am–12:30 am; Sun. 11:30 am–11:30 pm
(Open Sun. at 10 am during football season)

**WHEN DID YOU OPEN?**

Established 1997, reestablished 2004.

**WHAT ARE YOUR MOST POPULAR BEERS?**

Macadamia Nut Porter, Raspberry Lambic.

**WHICH BEERS ARE YOU PROUDEST OF?**

IPA. We've stayed true to tradition with an English style versus a West Coast style. It's well balanced but with a West Coast ABV and traditional hops— Cascade and Columbus.

**HAVE ANY OF YOUR BEERS WON AWARDS?**

GABF 2004, 2005; LA International Beer Fest 2016; Cal. State Fair 1997–2017; best of festivals (Davis, El Dorado Hills, Humboldt); and local awards (best brewery, best seasonal).

**WHAT ARE THE BIGGEST CHALLENGES YOUR BREWERY HAS FACED?**

Every day can be a challenge. We are a small brewery run by two women. We suffer burnout and exhaustion. We have to work daily to keep up with trends, stay relevant, and satisfy our customer base. Every day literally brings new challenges, but we wouldn't trade it for the world.

**WHAT'S THE ATMOSPHERE LIKE?**

We are lovingly known as the "Cheers" bar, where everybody knows your name and is always glad you came. We are also referred to as "the office" and as an "extended living room."

**DO YOU HAVE FOOD?**

We have a full pub menu featuring many locally made and organic products. We also offer a full bar featuring beer cocktails and house-infused spirits.

**WHAT ELSE CAN YOU TELL US?**

We are one of only three all-women-owned breweries in the state of California; two are located in Humboldt (Six Rivers and Lost Coast).

We are in a building built in 1926 on what used to be one of the biggest granite depositories in the country.

Because we have a view of the Mad River Valley and the Pacific Ocean, we are the Brew with a View. ❄

**3**

# MAD RIVER BREWING CO.

101 Taylor Way, Blue Lake, CA 95525
707-668-4151 • madriverbrewing.com

Sun.-Thurs. 11:30 am-9 pm;
Fri. & Sat. 11:30 am-10 pm

**WHEN DID YOU OPEN?**

1989.

**WHAT ARE YOUR MOST POPULAR BEERS?**

Steelhead Extra Pale Ale, Slammin' Salmon Double, Jamaica Red Ale.

**WHICH BEERS ARE YOU PROUDEST OF?**

We're proud of all of our beers. Each one is unique and flavorful in its own way.

**WHAT ARE THE BIGGEST CHALLENGES YOUR BREWERY HAS FACED?**

Financial, equipment, crowded markets, innovation; you name it.

**WHAT'S THE ATMOSPHERE LIKE?**

A bit of our own in-house "madness" coupled with a whole lot of bring-it-on!

**ARE YOU DOG & FAMILY FRIENDLY?**

Both!

**DO YOU HAVE FOOD?**

Yes.

**WHAT ELSE CAN YOU TELL US?**

We opened with Sierra Nevada's original brewing equipment and brewed on it for 27 years!

We were among the first 200 independent craft breweries in the U.S.

We listen to every kind of music, from Al Hirt to Zappa. ❄

# 4

# REDWOOD CURTAIN BREWING CO.

550 South G St., Suite 6, Arcata, CA 95521
707-826-7222 • redwoodcurtainbrewing.com

Sun.-Tues. noon-11 pm;
Wed.-Sat. noon-midnight

**WHEN DID YOU OPEN?**

April 2010.

**WHAT ARE YOUR MOST POPULAR BEERS?**

Imperial golden ales, India pale ales, our Funky Notion series (sour program), and specialty/rotating IPAs.

**WHICH BEERS ARE YOU PROUDEST OF?**

All of our beers. They are all brewed traditionally with four ingredients only: water, malt, hops, and yeast.

**HAVE ANY OF YOUR BEERS WON AWARDS?**

Special Bitter: bronze medal at 2016 GABF; Dusseldorf Altbier: silver medal at 2014 GABF.

**WHAT'S THE ATMOSPHERE LIKE?**

Some call us "the curtain." We have a community-oriented tasting room that is light and airy and a friendly and knowledgeable staff.

**ARE YOU DOG & FAMILY FRIENDLY?**

Family friendly.

**DO YOU HAVE FOOD?**

The LoCo Fish truck serves lunch and dinner seven days a week.

**WHAT ELSE CAN YOU TELL US?**

Family owned and operated since 2010. ❊

**5**

# LOST COAST BREWERY

Brewhouse taproom: 1600 Sunset Dr., Eureka, CA 95503
707-445-4484 • lostcoast.com

11 am–5 pm

Cafe & pub: 617 4th Street, Eureka, CA 95501
707-445-4480 • lostcoast.com

Sun.–Thurs. 11 am–10 pm;
Fri. & Sat. 11 am–11 pm

---

**WHEN DID YOU OPEN?**

1990.

**WHAT ARE YOUR MOST POPULAR BEERS?**

Great White, Tangerine Wheat, Fogcutter Double IPA.

---

**WHICH BEERS ARE YOU PROUDEST OF?**

Great White, Tangerine Wheat, Watermelon Wheat, and Fogcutter Double IPA. All are very unique flavors with unique graphics.

**HAVE ANY OF YOUR BEERS WON AWARDS?**

Yes, many. Nearly all of them have won something.

**WHAT ARE THE BIGGEST CHALLENGES YOUR BREWERY HAS FACED?**

Transitioning to a much larger production facility, launching our canning line, and providing beer internationally.

**WHAT'S THE ATMOSPHERE LIKE?**

Enthusiastic, energetic atmosphere with an age range across the board. We have killer beer.

**ARE YOU DOG & FAMILY FRIENDLY?**
The brewhouse taproom is both.

**DO YOU HAVE FOOD?**
Located in the heart of Old Town Eureka, we have a very diverse menu that appeals to all. We offer standard pub fare, a kids' menu, vegetarian dishes, and daily specials from our creative chef. We serve local grass-fed meats and the freshest seafood caught right off our coast.

**WHAT ELSE CAN YOU TELL US?**
Our brewhouse taproom has a gift shop, ice cream parlor, and hourly tours of the facility.

When Lost Coast brewed its first beer, there weren't a lot of craft breweries in existence, especially in California. Small batch brewing—or microbrewing—wasn't exactly a promising line of work, as few could take on the giants in the beer world.

What started as a crazy experiment soon grew into a fledgling brewery based out of a 100-year-old building in downtown Eureka. Funny things happen when you consistently crank out great beer. Lost Coast continued to expand, gaining fans around the globe and outgrowing a couple of brewing facilities along the way. We're now located just

south of Eureka, brewing out of a custom-built brewery that's designed to grow with the company. Currently, we can bottle and can up to 1.2 million beers and fill 1,400 kegs a day. But it's not just about volume; it's about efficiency as well. We use a state-of-the-art vapor condenser to turn the steam produced from boiling wort back into the hot water, which we use for the next brew. ✻

---

# The North
# and East

## THE NORTH

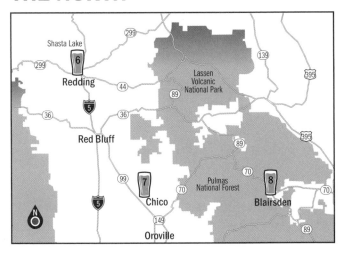

6. Woody's Brewing Co., Redding
7. Waganup Brewing, Chico
8. The Brewing Lair, Blairsden

# THE EAST

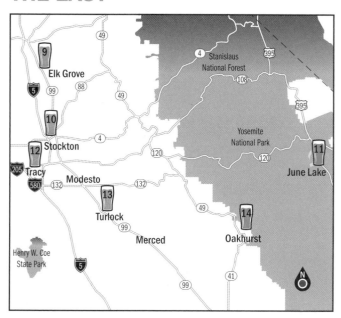

9. Flatland Brewing Co., Elk Grove
10. Channel Brewing Co., Stockton
11. June Lake Brewing, June Lake
12. Morgan Territory Brewing, Tracy
13. Dust Bowl Brewing Co., Turlock
14. South Gate Brewing Co., Oakhurst

**6**

# WOODY'S BREWING CO.

1257 Oregon St., Redding, CA 96001
530-768-1034 • Woodysbrewing.com

Tues.-Thurs. 11 am-10 pm; Fri. & Sat. 11 am-11 pm;
Sun. 11 am-9 pm

**WHEN DID YOU OPEN?**

January 2015.

**WHAT ARE YOUR MOST POPULAR BEERS?**

Our Chili Whit, Quickie West Coast IPA, Apricot Wheat, and our "buzz tap," which is a rotating beer with a higher ABV.

**WHICH OF YOUR BEERS ARE YOU PROUDEST OF AND WHY?**

This is not easily answered. I would say that our wheats and whit ales are something we are proud of. So many breweries nowadays are so hyped about IPAs and hops, but where's the love for everything else? We like to offer classic styles with some new, exciting creative ales.

**HAVE ANY OF YOUR BEERS WON AWARDS?**

Our Hopzerker, Swheat Dreams, Apricot Wheat, Teacher's Aide, and Porter have all won awards.

**WHAT ARE THE BIGGEST CHALLENGES YOUR BREWERY HAS FACED?**

The ever-increasing government regulations and increased competition. This is obviously a very popular industry to be in and has become harder over the years. The Brewers Association analyzed the market and found that it is in its maturity phase, which means it is fully saturated and we will start to see more breweries go out of business than go into business (which we are already starting to see).

**WHAT'S THE ATMOSPHERE LIKE?**

We are very laid-back. If you ask, customers will say they feel like they are at a friend's house. Customers feel like we are "real" and have a "comfortable vibe."

**ARE YOU DOG & FAMILY FRIENDLY?**

Family friendly, service dogs only.

**DO YOU HAVE FOOD?**

Yes, pub food. None of that fancy foo-foo stuff; this is real American-fusion pub food. We have won many awards for it, too!

**WHAT ELSE CAN YOU TELL US?**

We are family owned and operated: two brothers and one son. You will always see a family member on the floor or in the brewery because we are hands on.

Our name came from people's inability to pronounce our last name: Wlodarczyk, pronounced Wah-dar-check. People would try to pronounce it but never could, so they went with what they could say, which was "Wood," and then came the name "Woody." ❈

**7**

# WAGANUPA BREWING

1346 Longfellow Ave., Chico, CA 95926
530-259-3705 • waganupa.com

Wed.–Sat. 5–9 pm

**WHEN DID YOU OPEN?**

April 2015.

**WHAT ARE YOUR MOST POPULAR BEERS?**

Our most popular beer is probably the Rusty Squabbit Coffee Stout.

**HAVE ANY OF YOUR BEERS WON AWARDS?**

We have never entered our beers in a competition.

**WHAT ARE THE BIGGEST CHALLENGES YOUR BREWERY HAS FACED?**

The biggest challenge for Waganupa is the natural carbonation process. All our beers are 100 percent naturally carbonated in the keg by living yeast.

**WHAT'S THE ATMOSPHERE LIKE?**

The most common phrase we hear is how "comfortable and relaxing" our tasting rooms are.

**DO YOU HAVE FOOD?**

We encourage outside food. No kitchen at this time.

**WHAT ELSE CAN YOU TELL US?**

Waganupa (wa agnu p'a) was Ishi's name for Lassen Volcanic Peak; the Yahi translation was "center of the world."

We are an extremely small, three-barrel nanobrewery with very limited distribution. Our beers are rarely available outside of our tasting rooms. ❄

# THE BREWING LAIR

67007 CA Hwy. 70, Blairsden, CA 96103
530-394-0940 • thebrewinglair.com

Apr.–Dec. daily noon–8 pm;
Jan.–Mar. Fri.–Mon. noon–5 pm

**WHEN DID YOU OPEN?**

2011.

**WHAT ARE YOUR MOST POPULAR BEERS?**

Blair Belgian Blonde, Ambush IPA.

**WHICH BEERS ARE YOU PROUDEST OF?**

We love our Blair Belgian Blonde because it's very dry and slightly hoppy. Ambush IPA is a well-balanced West Coast IPA, with a slightly bready and big citrus hop flavor that everyone loves.

**WHAT ARE THE BIGGEST CHALLENGES YOUR BREWERY HAS FACED?**

The rain swelling up our little creek and washing out our culvert and driveway.

**WHAT'S THE ATMOSPHERE LIKE?**

We are "the best thing to happen in Plumas County since gold was found." We put a lot into our beautiful outdoor venue, which includes a big meadow and deck spaces, disc golf, Ping-Pong, cornhole, and a hiking trail.

**ARE YOU DOG & FAMILY FRIENDLY?**

Yes and yes.

**DO YOU HAVE FOOD?**

Locally made salami and kettle corn.

**WHAT ELSE CAN YOU TELL US?**

Our beer is made from well water.

We compost all our brewery waste and send the grain to feed local sheep.

We often have an equal ratio of kids and dogs to adults. ❄

# FLATLAND BREWING CO.

9183 Survey Rd., #104, Elk Grove, CA 95624
flatlandbrewingco.com

Thurs. & Fri. 3–9 pm;
Sat. noon–9 pm; Sun. noon–6 pm

**WHEN DID YOU OPEN?**
January 2016.

**WHAT ARE YOUR MOST POPULAR BEERS?**
IPAs—it doesn't matter the ABV, or hops, or style. Anything IPA!

**WHICH BEERS ARE YOU PROUDEST OF?**
Our barrel-aged sour beers, because of the time and attention that goes into them.

**HAVE ANY OF YOUR BEERS WON AWARDS?**
Second place at the Coffee Beer Fest West Coast Competition, (2016), People's Choice Award during Sac Beer Week (2017), and Best in Show at the Cal.

State Fair (2017).

**WHAT ARE THE BIGGEST CHALLENGES YOUR BREWERY HAS FACED?**
Keeping up with demand. We are small and people are thirsty.

**WHAT'S THE ATMOSPHERE LIKE?**
Cozy, comfortable, homey.

**DO YOU HAVE FOOD?**
No food, but food trucks do make it out.

**WHAT ELSE CAN YOU TELL US?**
We are always rotating beer, with no year-round offerings. Although our focus is in sour beer, we usually have an IPA or two to choose from. ✳

# CHANNEL BREWING CO.

110 N. San Joaquin St., Stockton, CA 95202
209-490-4928 • channelbrewing.co

Tues.–Thurs. 11 am–10 pm;
Fri. & Sat. 11 am–midnight

**WHEN DID YOU OPEN?**

March 2017.

**WHAT ARE YOUR MOST POPULAR BEERS?**

Smokey Scotch Ale and 209 Blonde Ale.

**WHICH BEERS ARE YOU PROUDEST OF?**

Big Pep Black IPA: great taste, and it is dedicated to the founder's grandfather.

**WHAT ARE THE BIGGEST CHALLENGES YOUR BREWERY HAS FACED?**

Getting people to come to the brewery at our downtown location. People still think there is nothing there.

**WHAT'S THE ATMOSPHERE LIKE?**

We have a clean and bright brewery where we encourage people to be a part of the community and embark on their own adventures. We have a 32-foot bar and a big community table. It's hard to sit by yourself here.

**ARE YOU DOG & FAMILY FRIENDLY?**

We are very family friendly (before 9 pm).

**DO YOU HAVE FOOD?**

We serve pizzas as well as some local wines.

**WHAT ELSE CAN YOU TELL US?**

We began our brewery with a successful Kickstarter campaign, raising $42,651 in 45 days!

We are the only microbrewery in Stockton.

We are all about experiencing the outdoors, and we enjoy things like backpacking, disc golf, and volleyball! ❋

# JUNE LAKE BREWING

131 S. Crawford Ave., June Lake, CA 93529
760-648-8000 • junelakebrewing.com

Daily 11 am–8 pm (summer); noon–8 pm (winter)

Archimedes Red Ale

**WHEN DID YOU OPEN?**

2014.

**WHAT ARE YOUR MOST POPULAR BEERS?**

Hutte DIPA, Lil' Walker IPA, Sasquatchito XPA, Deer Beer Brown Ale, Silver Lake Saison.

**WHICH BEERS ARE YOU PROUDEST OF?**

Our seasonal GullllLager because it's a super clean, low-alcohol American-style lager that we dry hop like an IPA.

**WHAT ARE THE BIGGEST CHALLENGES YOUR BREWERY HAS FACED?**

The difficulties of getting raw materials and equipment shipped to us. Our closest Home Depot is 120 miles away (one way) and located in another state.

**WHAT'S THE ATMOSPHERE LIKE?**

We're known as the punk rock/metal brewery. We do not play

sports or take music requests. It's all about the beer and your interactions with other like-minded humans.

### ARE YOU DOG & FAMILY FRIENDLY?

Yes, if they (kids and dogs) do not bite, bark, urinate, or defecate and they are on tended leashes.

### DO YOU HAVE FOOD?

Our friends operate a food truck, called Ohanas 395, in our parking lot that serves awaiian fusion food from 11 am to 4 pm.

### WHAT ELSE CAN YOU TELL US?

Super awesome beer is number one, employees are number two, and customers are number three. Our mission statement is to make super awesome beer, get people outside, and give back to our community.

Our tasting room floor comprises around $1,200 in change (primarily pennies) covered in epoxy.

We did all the construction and buildout for our location, including hanging the 8,140 square feet of drywall. ❖

# MORGAN TERRITORY BREWING

1885 N. MacArthur Dr., Tracy, CA 95376

209-834-8664 • morganterritorybrewing.com

Wed.–Fri. 2–9 pm;  Sat. & Sun. noon–9 pm

**WHEN DID YOU OPEN?**

March 2016.

**WHAT ARE YOUR MOST POPULAR BEERS?**

IPAs constitute the majority of the sales, with all other styles being relatively evenly distributed.

**WHICH BEERS ARE YOU PROUDEST OF?**

Dead Reckoning Imperial Porter—it is recently our most successful beer, winning a gold medal at the World Beer Cup and a silver medal at the GABF. It was known as Apogee Baltic porter before we were forced to change the name over a trademark dispute. Grinding Stone Oatmeal Stout is our most decorated beer, winning multiple medals over the years at the World Beer Cup and GABF. Old Diablo Barley Wine—if there is a beer that we are most known for among other brewers and breweries, it would

be our barley wine. It's hard to describe a better feeling than being recognized by your peers. This is the style we get asked the most questions about how we make it.

**HAVE ANY OF YOUR OTHER BEERS WON AWARDS?**

Yes, many of our beers have won awards. A list of awards can be seen on our website.

**WHAT ARE THE BIGGEST CHALLENGES YOUR BREWERY HAS FACED?**

Not enough hours in the day to get everything done. We are a small operation, and everyone who works here is spread thin in terms of their abilities to get everything done that running a brewery entails, i.e., brewing, tasting room, marketing, events, sales, accounting, accounts receivable and payable. Everyone wears many hats here. I have the glamorous title of owner on my business card, but I am also bartender, janitor, bathroom attendant, and keg washer.

### WHAT'S THE ATMOSPHERE LIKE?

The brewery itself is clean and well laid out to accommodate growth without delays in production as we grow. The tasting room is very inviting and features reclaimed wood from an old horse stable, an awning over the bar top, four TVs for sporting events, and a back area that is used as an overflow area and for small private parties. The vibe is rustic, with an atmosphere that pays homage to Tracy's agricultural history.

### DO YOU HAVE FOOD?

Customers are encouraged to bring their own food, have it delivered, or purchase it from the food trucks that are here from time to time. Many of our customers tailgate in the parking lot. They cook their food outside on their own grills and bring their food inside to eat. No drinking is permitted in the parking lot, so we are working with the city to get some patio space where people can enjoy a beer outdoors as they barbecue.

### WHAT ELSE CAN YOU TELL US?

We used to be Schooner's Grille & Brewery in Antioch. Technically, we still are, with the same LLC, owners, brewmaster (now an owner as well), and beer recipes. We changed our name because another brewery trademarked Schooner's. We are the original, but by the time we looked into trademarks, we had missed a five-year window to contest the other Schooner. We rebranded when we moved as Morgan Territory Brewing. Morgan Territory is a park on the East Side of Mount Diablo, roughly halfway between Tracy and Antioch.

Craig Cauwels is the brewmaster and now an owner. He is one of the most decorated brewers in the country in terms of awards—he has won a medal at the GABF every year that he has entered a beer! He led a team of scientists doing cancer research at Harvard University before he became a brewer. Because of his background, he is extremely process oriented, with meticulous attention to detail.

The opening of our tasting room was Friday May 13, 2016. Some may say Friday the 13th is an unlucky day to open, but we just couldn't wait any longer. You want your opening to be perfect, but the fact of the matter is, perfect doesn't ever happen, and at some point, you just have to open. So far so good. Our favorite online review is on Yelp. It reads something like "Morgan Territory Brewing is the best thing to happen to Tracy since Costco came here." ✳

# DUST BOWL BREWING CO.

Taproom: 200 Main St., Turlock, CA 95380
209-250-2043 • dustbowlbrewing.com

Tues.-Thurs. 11 am-10 pm;
Fri. & Sat. 11 am-11 pm; Sun. 11 am-9 pm

Brewery: 3000 Fulkerth Rd., Turlock, CA 95380
209-250-2042 • dustbowlbrewing.com

Sun.-Thurs. 11 am-9 pm;
Fri. & Sat. 11 am-10 pm

**WHEN DID YOU OPEN?**
2009.

**WHAT ARE YOUR MOST POPULAR BEERS?**
Hops of Wrath IPA and Taco Truck Lager.

**WHICH BEERS ARE YOU PROUDEST OF?**
We'd have to say Hops of Wrath IPA. This was the first beer we brewed and kegged for sale to the public. Hops of Wrath gave us our footing in the craft beer industry. It was well received and continues to be a top seller for us. The name was memorable, which was intentional then and even more important now—there's a lot of good craft beer on the market. You have to provide a total experience for the consumer—the beer, the name, the imagery—it all goes hand in hand. It's not enough anymore to just have a good beer, the competition is too stiff.

**HAVE ANY OF YOUR BEERS WON AWARDS?**
Too many to list here!

**WHAT ARE THE BIGGEST CHALLENGES YOUR BREWERY HAS FACED?**
When we launched Dust Bowl Brewing Co., the biggest challenge was building brand awareness and establishing a craft beer culture in our hometown. Once we accomplished that, we continued to run out of capacity despite continual expansions.

We made a huge leap in 2016 with the investment in and opening of a new brewery and a second taproom. Today's biggest challenges are growing our sales footprint, expanding production, and managing more than 150 employees.

WHAT'S THE ATMOSPHERE LIKE?

The taproom has a very cool vibe. The decor is industrial chic, featuring the talents of many local businesses and artisans. The taproom features floor-to-ceiling window views into the brewery, two 20-tap towers, indoor and outdoor dining, a beer garden, outdoor games (bocce courts, cornhole, giant Jenga, giant Connect Four), and event spaces. We also offer tours.

**ARE YOU DOG & FAMILY FRIENDLY?**

Both locations are family friendly.

**DO YOU HAVE FOOD?**

Modern pub fare. Some favorites include fried squeakers (cheese curds), ahi poke, burgers, pizzas, fish tacos, fresh salads, home-made soups, and house-made desserts.

**WHAT ELSE CAN YOU TELL US?**

The founder, Brett Tate, is a retired teacher who created the brewery in his mind—the brewery name, the history, the beer names, etc.—but he had never been a homebrewer. His dream came to life when he read about Don Oliver, a local homebrewer who had won the Samuel Adams National Longshot Homebrew Contest. Brett arranged a meeting with Don, and the rest is history, as the saying goes.

Most of the beer names tie back to Brett's family heritage as migrant Okies who made their way west into California during the Dust Bowl era. Hops of Wrath, California Line, Public Enemy, Great Impression, and Black Blizzard are a few of the names that harken to the company's roots. ✳

14

# SOUTH GATE BREWING CO.

40233 Enterprise Dr., Oakhurst, CA 93644
559-692-2739 • southgatebrewco.com

Sun.–Thurs. 11 am–9 pm; Fri. & Sat. 11 am–10 pm
(Closing hours may vary with the season)

**WHEN DID YOU OPEN?**
May 2013.

**WHAT ARE YOUR MOST POPULAR BEERS?**
South Gate IPA, Gold Diggin' Blonde Ale, Deadwood Porter. Our seasonal and specialty beers are favorites as well and usually go quickly.

**WHICH BEERS ARE YOU PROUDEST OF?**
Brewmaster Rick Boucke is most proud of the Oaktown Pecan Brown. It is widely loved and appeals to light and dark beer drinkers alike. With pecan and maple characteristics, it is truly one of a kind.

**HAVE ANY OF YOUR BEERS WON AWARDS?**
Oaktown Pecan Brown: gold at San Diego International Beer Festival and gold at NorCal Brew Competition; Tomahawk Imperial Red: gold at the LA International Beer Festival; Brooklyn Imperial Stout: gold at NorCal Brew Competition; Bob Barley: gold at NorCal Brew Competition.

**WHAT ARE THE BIGGEST CHALLENGES YOUR BREWERY HAS FACED?**
Supply and demand. As of 2017, we maximized our five-barrel system to its fullest potential and still had to keep our wholesale customer base small. We look forward to a brewery expansion in the coming year or two.

**WHAT'S THE ATMOSPHERE LIKE?**
Boutique, industrial chic; the attached restaurant is rich with reclaimed wood and cool touches and fixtures. Vibe is warm, neighborly, and inviting.

**ARE YOU DOG & FAMILY FRIENDLY?**
Kids yes; dogs no.

## Do you have food?

Classic and elevated pub fare, thoughtfully sourced, utilizing organic, local, and seasonal ingredients as much as possible. We use local farmers' produce often. Burgers are made with grass-fed beef; sauces and dressings are made in-house. Favorites include fish and chips, bangers and mash, and house-made black bean burgers. Fresh catch of the day is popular as well.

## What else can you tell us?

The building was previously a car dealership. The owners completely revamped it into a brewery and restaurant.

The restaurant doubled its size in 2016.

The food menu changes about every six months.

We carry our own beers as well as an exciting list of other craft brews on tap and by the bottle, and we have a great wine list. ✳

# On (and Off)
# I-80

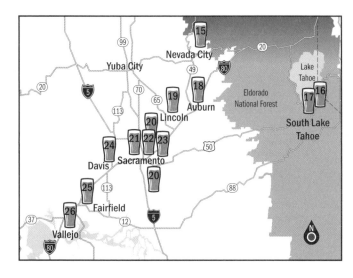

15. Three Forks Bakery & Brewing Co., Nevada City
16. The Brewery at Lake Tahoe, South Lake Tahoe
17. Sidellis Lake Tahoe, South Lake Tahoe
18. Moonraker Brewing Co., Auburn
19. GoatHouse Brewing Co., Lincoln
20. Track 7 Brewing Co., 826 Professor Lane, Sacramento
20. Track 7 Brewing Co., 3747 W Pacific Ave., Sacramento
21. Yolo Brewing Co., 1520 Terminal St., West Sacramento
22. Hoppy Brewing Co., 2425 24th St., Sacramento
23. Sactown Union Brewery, 1210 66th St., Sacramento
24. Three Mile Brewing Co., Davis
25. Heretic Brewing Co., Fairfield
26. Mare Island Brewing Co., Vallejo

**15**

# THREE FORKS BAKERY & BREWING CO.

211 Commercial St., Nevada City, CA 95959
530-470-8333 • threeforksnc.com

Mon., Wed., Thurs. 7 am–10 pm; Fri. 7 am–11 pm;
Sat. 8 am–11 pm; Sun. 8 am–10 pm

**WHEN DID YOU OPEN?**
August 2014.

**WHAT ARE YOUR MOST POPULAR BEERS?**
Emerald Pool IPA, Oak Tree Pale Ale, Dynamite Double IPA, Mother's Beach Blonde, Purdon Porter.

**WHICH BEERS ARE YOU PROUDEST OF?**
We're proud of our Dynamite Double IPA for capturing the hoppiness of an imperial IPA but

having a clean and dry balance. We're proud of Oak Tree Pale Ale as a refreshing pale ale with a nice citrus burst from Amarillo hops but well balanced.

**Have any of your beers won awards?**

Dynamite Double IPA won a gold in the 2016 California Commercial Beer competition at the Cal. State Fair.

**What are the biggest challenges your brewery has faced?**

As a small brewhouse, keeping up with demand has at times been challenging.

**What's the atmosphere like?**

We have an open, bright, inviting space. Our brewpub has a small-town feel with lots of people meeting up and making new friends as a result of our communal seating.

**Do you have food?**

We serve wood-fired pizza, soup, salad, and sandwiches, and we are also an artisan bakery. We make just about everything we serve from scratch, including all of our breads, sauces, and condiments and many of our cured meats. We source all of our meat and eggs and most of our produce locally.

**What else can you tell us?**

We are named for the three forks of the Yuba River (north, south, and middle), and most of our beers are named for our favorite places on the river. ❀

# THE BREWERY AT LAKE TAHOE

3542 Lake Tahoe Blvd., South Lake Tahoe, CA 96150
530-544-2739 • brewerylaketahoe.com

Open daily at 11 am

**WHEN DID YOU OPEN?**
December 1992.

**WHAT ARE YOUR MOST POPULAR BEERS?**
Bad Ass Ale.

**WHICH BEERS ARE YOU PROUDEST OF?**
We keep seven of our brews on tap at all times, with additional seasonal offerings such as Peanut Butter Porter or Double Vision Double IPA.

**WHAT'S THE ATMOSPHERE LIKE?**
Casual brewpub with patio dining in summer, fireside dining in winter. Our customers have said that our brews, food, and service are "awesome" and "bomb."

**DO YOU HAVE FOOD?**
We have a wide variety, with burgers, salads, BBQ ribs, pizzas, pastas, sandwiches, and appetizers.

**WHAT ELSE CAN YOU TELL US?**
We are Tahoe's original brewery, launched more than 25 years ago and still brewing strong. ✳

**17**

# SIDELLIS LAKE TAHOE

3350 Sandy Way, South Lake Tahoe, CA 96150
530-600-3999 • sidellis.com

Sun.–Thurs. 11:30 am–9:30 pm;
Fri. & Sat. 11:30 am–10:30 pm

**WHEN DID YOU OPEN?**
January 2016.

**WHAT ARE YOUR MOST POPULAR BEERS?**
Brewocracy IPA and Clockwork White.

**WHICH BEERS ARE YOU PROUDEST OF?**
Our barrel-aged sour program.

**WHAT ARE THE BIGGEST CHALLENGES YOUR BREWERY HAS FACED?**
Keeping up.

**WHAT'S THE ATMOSPHERE LIKE?**
Summer outdoor beer garden. Inside, industrial cabin look.

**DO YOU HAVE FOOD?**
Sandwiches, salads, appetizers.

**WHAT ELSE CAN YOU TELL US?**
Employee owned.

The name Sidellis is a contraction of the last names of owner Chris Sidell and his husband Ellwood Ellis. ❋

# MOONRAKER BREWING CO.

12970 Earhart Ave., Suite 100, Auburn, CA 95602
530-745-6816 • moonrakerbrewing.com

Wed.-Fri. 3-9pm;
Sat. noon-9 pm; Sun. noon-8 pm

**WHEN DID YOU OPEN?**
Earth Day 2016.

**WHAT ARE YOUR MOST POPULAR BEERS?**

New England–style IPAs; we are best known for Yojo/Dojo.

**WHICH BEERS ARE YOU PROUDEST OF?**

Yojo/Dojo was one of the first Northern California–brewed New England–style IPAs. It put us on the map.

**HAVE ANY OF YOUR BEERS WON AWARDS?**

Yojo/Dojo: one of the top 50 beers in the world according to RateBeer. Miss Conduct: gold at the 2016 Cal. State Fair and silver at the 2016 GABF. Vespers Nine: gold at the 2016 U.S. Open. Mosaic Crush: gold at the 2017 San Diego International Beer Festival. Wicked Whisper: gold at the 2017 Cal. State Fair. All Hops on Deck: silver at the

2017 Cal. State Fair. Goofy Foot: silver at the 2017 Cal. State Fair. Citra Crush: bronze at the 2017 Cal. State Fair.

**WHAT ARE THE BIGGEST CHALLENGES YOUR BREWERY HAS FACED?**

Keeping up with demand.

**WHAT'S THE ATMOSPHERE LIKE?**

Cool vibe.

**ARE YOU DOG & FAMILY FRIENDLY?**

Yes and yes.

**DO YOU HAVE FOOD?**

We have rotating food trucks on the days we are open.

**WHAT ELSE CAN YOU TELL US?**

In 2016, we were named Best New Brewery in California and ninth Best New Brewery in the World by RateBeer.

We were one of the first Northern California breweries to make a New England–style "juicy" beer and put it in a 16-ounce can. ❊

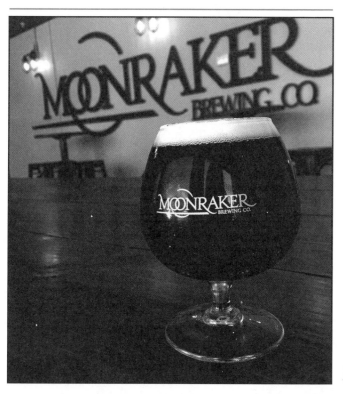

19

# GOATHOUSE BREWING CO.

600 Wise Rd., Lincoln, CA 95648
916-740-9100 • goathousebrewing.com

Thurs. & Fri. 2–6 pm;
Sat. & Sun. 11 am–6 pm

**WHEN DID YOU OPEN?**
September 2013.

**WHAT ARE YOUR MOST POPULAR BEERS?**
Our beer is 99 percent seasonal and tied to what is local, fresh, and available. For example, when mandarins are ready on our farm, we make mandarin beer; when they are finished, the beer is not available. We don't use extracts out of season.

**WHICH BEERS ARE YOU PROUDEST OF?**
All of them.

**WHAT ARE THE BIGGEST CHALLENGES YOUR BREWERY HAS FACED?**
Being one of the only true farm-to-tap breweries—where the farming and brewing happen on the same land—in the state of California has been challenging because the government isn't re-ally set up for innovation or the unknown.

**WHAT'S THE ATMOSPHERE LIKE?**
We grow 20 different varietals of hops on-site (more than 1,200 plants); we have orchards and gardens; and we work with two beekeepers for on-site hop honey. And yes, we do have goats (and a dairy may or may not be in our future)!

**ARE YOU DOG & FAMILY FRIENDLY?**
Supervised children and dogs on leashes are welcome!

**DO YOU HAVE FOOD?**
No.

**WHAT ELSE CAN YOU TELL US?**
GoatHouse Brewing offers "farm yoga," yoga with our goats and donkey, in the pasture behind the brewery and hop fields! Beer does follow the yoga session! ❄

# TRACK 7 BREWING CO.

3747 W. Pacific Ave., Suite F, Sacramento, CA 95829;
826 Professor Lane, Suite 100, Sacramento, CA 95834
916-520-4677 • track7brewing.com

Summer: Mon.-Wed. 3-9 pm; Thurs. 3-10 pm;
Fri. & Sat. noon-10 pm; Sun. noon-9 pm
Rest of year: Mon.-Thurs. 3-9 pm; Fri.-Sun. noon-9 pm

**WHEN DID YOU OPEN?**
2011.

**WHAT ARE YOUR MOST POPULAR BEERS?**
Panic IPA, Left Eye Right Eye Double IPA.

**WHICH BEERS ARE YOU PROUDEST OF?**
Our beers are like our kids, we love them all!

**HAVE ANY OF YOUR BEERS WON AWARDS?**
We have won a number of awards. Our biggest award to date is silver at GABF for our Hoppy Palm in the American Pale Ale category.

**WHAT ARE THE BIGGEST CHALLENGES YOUR BREWERY HAS FACED?**
Keeping up with the various demands.

**WHAT'S THE ATMOSPHERE LIKE?**
Industrial park chic.

**DO YOU HAVE FOOD?**
Food trucks at both breweries every day.

**WHAT ELSE CAN YOU TELL US?**
Governor Jerry Brown signed the legislation allowing growler fills in any growler, subject to certain labeling provisions, at our Curtis Park brewery. ❋

**21**

# YOLO BREWING CO.

1520 Terminal St., West Sacramento, CA 95691
916-379-7581 • yolobrew.com

Tues. & Wed. 4–9 pm; Thurs. 3–9 pm; Fri. 3–10 pm;
Sat. 11 am–10 pm; Sun. 11 am–6 pm

**WHEN DID YOU OPEN?**
June 2014.

**WHAT ARE YOUR MOST POPULAR BEERS?**
Colossus Double IPA, Orange Blossom Blonde, Nutty Brown.

**HAVE ANY OF YOUR BEERS WON AWARDS?**
Nutty Brown Ale took gold in the 2016 Cal. State Fair for English brown ales. Cousins Mexican Porter has also won awards.

**WHAT ARE THE BIGGEST CHALLENGES YOUR BREWERY HAS FACED?**
As with any business, we have had our challenges in finding the right crew members who share our vision and who are passionate and driven about what they do. We made lots of changes recently, and we are thrilled with our team, the beer we are making, and the direction we are heading in.

**WHAT'S THE ATMOSPHERE LIKE?**
Our beer hall is spacious, family friendly, and extremely laid-back. On a typical day you can find families enjoying a meal together, couples of all ages on dates, and hardworking professionals enjoying a cold one after work. We try hard to offer a variety of activities that bring the community together and give everyone the chance to get to know their neighbors a bit better, including trivia on Tuesdays, cornhole leagues on Wednesdays, live local musicians on Fridays and Saturdays, and free yoga classes on Sunday mornings.

**ARE YOU DOG & FAMILY FRIENDLY?**
Yes.

## Do you have food?

We do not have a kitchen (we prefer to focus on the beer), but we do make sure that there is a food truck parked right out front every day that we are open. Don't drink on an empty stomach!

## What else can you tell us?

We offer personal brewing sessions to anyone interested in brewing! Our brewers guide you through the process of making your very own custom brew. Brew, bottle, drink, repeat!

We have an extremely large taproom that is the perfect space for parties and events! We host everything from birthday parties to company team-building days. ❋

**22**

# HOPPY BREWING CO.

2425 24th St., Sacramento, CA 95818
916-451-4677 • hoppy.com

Mon.-Wed. 11 am-midnight; Thurs. & Fri. 11 am-1 am;
Sat. 10 am-1 am; Sun. 10 am-midnight

**WHEN DID YOU OPEN?**

We poured our first beers July 1994 in San Jose, but we didn't open our brick-and-mortar until June 1999 in Sacramento.

**WHAT ARE YOUR MOST POPULAR BEERS?**

Our bottled beers are the most popular: Liquid Sunshine Blond Ale, Hoppy Face Amber Ale, Stony Face Red Ale, Hoppy Claus Holiday Ale, and Total Eclipse Black Ale.

**HAVE ANY OF YOUR BEERS WON AWARDS?**

Yes, the Hoppy Face Amber Ale, Total Eclipse Black Ale, and Hoppy Claus Holiday Ale have all been big winners.

**WHAT ARE THE BIGGEST CHALLENGES YOUR BREWERY HAS FACED?**

The ups and downs of the industry have always been a challenge;

this current surge is different than we have seen in the past.

**WHAT'S THE ATMOSPHERE LIKE?**

Without trying to be everything to everybody, there is something for all. We have several TVs, and we purchase the NFL, NBA,

time; we have a fireplace room (with A/V capabilities) that can be closed off for privacy.

**WHAT ELSE CAN YOU TELL US ABOUT YOUR BREWERY?**

Over the years, we've been distributed in about 25 states.

One of the original members of our team is now brewing Hoppy Face Amber Ale in the Czech Republic.

We are excited that we are served in the Golden 1 Center and Papa Murphy's Park (venues where professional sports teams play). ✳

and NHL packages. We have a little bit of live music. We have two "hoppy" hours daily and all-day Monday. We are near SMUD (the local utility company); the University of California, Davis, teaching hospital; and Sacramento State University.

**ARE YOU DOG & FAMILY FRIENDLY?**

We have an outdoor patio for the pooches and a kids' menu that includes $1 kids' meals a couple of days a week.

**DO YOU HAVE FOOD?**

We are a brewpub and seat more than 100 guests at a

# SACTOWN UNION BREWERY

1210 66th St., Unit B, Sacramento, CA 95819
916-272-4IPA (4472) • SactownUnion.com

Mon-Thurs. 4-10 pm; Fri. 2-11 pm;
Sat. noon-11 pm; Sun. noon-8 pm (Beer Yoga Sun. at 10:30 am)

**WHEN DID YOU OPEN?**

2016.

**WHAT ARE YOUR MOST POPULAR BEERS?**

Something Wicked IPA and #KöLSCH Köln-style Ale.

**WHICH BEERS ARE YOU PROUDEST OF?**

That's a tough question! Like picking a favorite kid! Overall, I am proudest of our wide range of styles, all brewed to be clean, authentic, and consistent and brewed to style. Where many breweries nowadays do 20 IPAs and a porter, we have a broad array to choose from—from our First Responder Helles Lager and Ode'Leia Mexican Lager to The Catalyst Sacramento Common (a handwritten recipe from 1853 we found in the city archives), to our Centennial Falcon West Coast Pale Ale, to our Something Wicked IPA and Prop 64 Session IPA and our I'm an IPA Guy! series of single-hopped IPAs, all the way to our Carpe Noctem Oatmeal Coffee Stout (with coffee from Chocolate Fish Coffee Roasters here in East Sac) and our Diamond in an Ice Storm Imperial Stout. We've got all the bases covered!

**HAVE ANY OF YOUR BEERS WON AWARDS?**

#KöLSCH Köln-style Ale, The Catalyst Sacramento Common, Centennial Falcon West Coast Pale Ale, and Jeff's Hefe have each won many. Our Lando Cascadian Dark Ale took first prize at last year's West Coast Coffee Beer Fest Competition.

**WHAT ARE THE BIGGEST CHALLENGES YOUR BREWERY HAS FACED?**

We had a number of unexpected hurdles to overcome just getting open—from city permit and licensing headaches to a crooked contractor. But since opening, the biggest challenge has been keeping up with demand! We are literally selling it as fast as we can brew it, and the demands that puts on cash flow (ordering more raw materials in time to brew the next batch, while waiting for retailers to send in payment) can sometimes put us in a pinch.

### What's the atmosphere like?

We've always wanted our brewery to feel warm, welcoming, inviting—as much a community center where people come to congregate as a place to try a new beer or get a growler fill. Our company ethos is "We're not just brewing beer; we're brewing community," and that ethos pervades through everything we do. From the local art and pictures of the pioneers of the craft brewing movement that adorn our walls to the nonprofit fundraiser and community-building events we host here, that belief is a very important part of who we are. We have a huge HD movie screen on our wall showing all the sports games, and we have events like game nights on Tuesday, pub trivia on Wednesday, cornhole tournaments on Thursday, and Beer Yoga on Sunday.

### Are you dog & family friendly?

We're very dog friendly; kid friendly until 8 pm.

### Do you have food?

We have a different food truck here every Wednesday through Sunday night. We also have some snacks and sodas available.

### What else can you tell us?

Our cofounder/brewmaster Michael Barker has been brewing commercially for more than 20 years and has won gold medals at the GABF and at the World Beer Cup.

Each beer in our Revolutionaries series is brewed in honor of a different social catalyst—a person or group who has worked to make our community better—and has a built-in contribution to a local nonprofit associated with the person/group that each beer is brewed in honor of.

We recently started releasing canned beer! This is a big turning point in our growth' and we're very excited to see where the next steps lead us! ❄

**24**

# THREE MILE BREWING CO.

231 G St., Suite 3, Davis, CA 95616
530-564-4351 • threemilebrewing.com

Wed.-Fri. 3-10 pm;
Sat. noon-10 pm; Sun. noon-8 pm

**WHEN DID YOU OPEN?**

February 2015.

**WHAT ARE YOUR MOST POPULAR BEERS?**

Our taps rotate frequently, but one of the classics that has stayed on due to overwhelming customer demand is the New Dog IPA, one of the first beers we created highlighting Citra hops. Big citrus and tropical fruit flavors make this beer a solid customer favorite.

**WHICH BEERS ARE YOU PROUDEST OF?**

We are proud of every single beer we create, but one of the ones that we are very proud of is our Hibiscus Honey Blonde. This beer is brewed using locally sourced honey infused with hibiscus flowers and pours into a glass with a gorgeous deep pink hue. It tastes tart and crisp, with a slight honey-hibiscus nose. It's a unique and very fun beer to make and drink.

**HAVE ANY OF YOUR BEERS WON AWARDS?**

At the 2017 Cal. State Fair we took home a bronze for our Portland Dark Scottish Ale and a gold for our Momosaic Pale Ale.

**WHAT ARE THE BIGGEST CHALLENGES YOUR BREWERY HAS FACED?**

We are fortunate that we haven't had any major challenges. We're a great team that really knows how to pull together to get the job done. There are seven founders of Three Mile, and each one brings something different and critically valuable to the group.

**WHAT'S THE ATMOSPHERE LIKE?**

When we initially sat down to "capture the dream" of opening a

brewery and taproom, we aligned on one overarching theme: to provide a welcoming place to drink world-class craft beer. We are relaxed and informal—bring kids, bring food, hang out, have fun. What we will never relax is the standard of quality for our beer. We put the utmost care and attention to detail into every single pint of beer that is brewed and poured.

**ARE YOU DOG & FAMILY FRIENDLY?**

Family friendly.

**DO YOU HAVE FOOD?**

We don't serve food, but we are very fortunate to be located in downtown Davis, where great restaurants are abundant. Many of these restaurants will deliver food to your table at Three Mile, and customers are encouraged to bring food in with them if they so desire. We've had people bring in everything from wedding cakes to charcuterie.

**WHAT ELSE CAN YOU TELL US?**

Everyone wants to know about the name Three Mile Brewing Co. and how we settled on that. It has absolutely nothing to do with islands or Eminem—it's a reference to a ban that the California State Legislature enacted in 1911. This ban prevented the sale of all alcoholic beverages within a three-mile radius of the UC campus, with the intent of preventing the corruption of young farming students at the university. This ban stood until 1979, almost 50 years after the repeal of Prohibition! ❋

**25**

# HERETIC BREWING CO.

1052 Horizon Dr., Suite B, Fairfield, CA 94533
707-389-4573 • hereticbrewing.com

Mon.-Thurs. 3-9 pm;
Fri.-Sun. noon-9 pm

**WHEN DID YOU OPEN?**

June 2011.

**WHAT ARE YOUR MOST POPULAR BEERS?**

Evil Twin Red IPA, Evil Cousin Double IPA, Chocolate Hazelnut Porter, German helles lagers, and our rotating fruit sours.

**WHICH BEERS ARE YOU PROUDEST OF?**

The lager is absolutely on point; it's crisp, clean, and refreshing. It takes longer to make a great lager, and so more things have the opportunity to go awry.

**HAVE ANY OF YOUR BEERS WON AWARDS?**

We have won many gold, silver, and bronze medals from competitions all over the world.

**WHAT ARE THE BIGGEST CHALLENGES YOUR BREWERY HAS FACED?**

In the beginning, it was growing pains; we couldn't keep up with demand. Now it's running a

large facility and the hundreds of moving parts that keep it going.

### WHAT'S THE ATMOSPHERE LIKE?

We are a casual, kick back and relax kind of place. Watch sports or strike up a conversation with a stranger or a new friend. We have board games, cards, crayons, and books for kids and adults alike. Our motto is "Be a heretic. Don't drink ordinary beer."

### ARE YOU DOG & FAMILY FRIENDLY?

Family friendly.

### DO YOU HAVE FOOD?

We offer snacks such as pretzels, and we often have food trucks on the weekend.

### WHAT ELSE CAN YOU TELL US?

Our brewery is family owned and was started by Jamil Zainasheff, a well-known homebrewing author, radio personality, and award-winning brewer. Jamil, his wife Liz, and their daughters are hands on with every aspect of the brewery.

Due to Jamil's homebrewing audience, he can send word out if he needs help. Before there was Uber or Lyft, he was on a road trip in our old RV and got stranded in Greeley, CO. He sent out a tweet that he needed a ride from "the only beater RV in the park" to a place in town, and within five minutes a guy responded that he'd be over to pick Jamil up in ten minutes. The homebrew community is full of big-hearted, generous folks, and we have loved being part of that community for almost two decades.

Liz and Jamil's daughter Anisa works in the taproom. At least once a week, a customer in the taproom asks her if she listens to her dad's radio shows. She typically responds that she hears him enough without having to also listen to him on the podcasts. ❈

# MARE ISLAND BREWING CO.

289 Mare Island Way, Vallejo, CA 94590
707-649-1200 • mareislandbrewingco.com

Daily 11:30 am – 10 pm

**WHAT ARE YOUR MOST POPULAR BEERS?**

Saginaw Golden Ale—a beer that has intensity without too much weight. Delicate malt flavor, a hint of citrus and floral notes, and lively effervescence make this the perfect accompaniment to a summer barbecue … or almost any meal! Hydraulic Sandwich IPA is a judicious interpretation of the IPA style, with glorious hop aromatics and sufficient bitterness, but reserved enough to allow the malt to show through (as it should).

**WHICH BEERS ARE YOU PROUDEST OF?**

Our flagship brew is the General Order No. 99, which is our finest porter recipe, aged for 6–12 months in former whiskey and pinot noir oak barrels, and bottled with cork and cage. It's an amazing blend of power and finesse.

### What are the biggest challenges your brewery has faced?

We've been building our new brewery for over three years—we're completely restoring a former coal shed on Mare Island (where coal was stored for the Navy's steamships in the early 1900s). It's been a project of vast scope and unbelievable challenges. But we're finally up and brewing amid all that history.

### What's the atmosphere like?

Just a beautiful 45-minute ferry ride from San Francisco or a 5-minute drive off the I-80, our taproom sits right on the water at the ferry landing in Vallejo, with a sweeping view of Mare Island and the Mare Island Strait through picture windows. Our taproom hosts live acoustic music, has HD television screens, and has one of the best patios and upstairs outdoor observation decks around.

### Are you dog & family friendly?

Yes and yes.

### Do you have food?

We offer a simple gourmet menu with daily specials, live acoustic music acts, wine, and, oh, beer, we have beer.

### What else can you tell us?

Our taproom is filled with Mare Island history. The walls are from lumber reclaimed when the old laundry building was demolished on Mare Island. The tables used to be the walls of the coal shed. We have artifacts from Mare Island that make the local museum jealous. A part of our mission is to spread the word about the incredible heritage of Mare Island and its contribution to the history and freedom of our country. Although the island may no longer craft battleships, we do now craft beer! ❄

# Wine Country

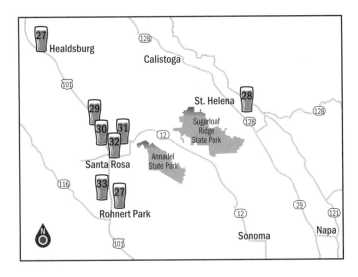

27. Bear Republic Brewing Co., Healdsburg
27. Bear Republic Brewing Co., Rohnert Park
28. Mad Fritz, St. Helena
29. Moonlight Brewing Co., 3350 Coffey Lane, Santa Rosa
30. Fogbelt Brewing Co., 1305 Cleveland Ave., Santa Rosa
31. Russian River Brewing Co., 725 4th St., Santa Rosa
32. Third Street Aleworks, 601, 3rd St., Santa Rosa
33. HenHouse Brewing Co., 322 Bellevue Ave., Santa Rosa

# BEAR REPUBLIC BREWING CO.

345 Healdsburg Ave., Healdsburg, CA 95448
5000 Roberts Lake Rd., Rohnert Park, CA 94928
707-433-2337 • bearrepublic.com

Healdsburg: Sun.–Thurs. 11 am–9 pm; Fri. & Sat. 11 am–9:30 pm

Rohnert Park: Sun–Thurs. 11 am–9 pm; Fri. & Sat. 11 am–midnight

**WHEN DID YOU OPEN?**
1996.

**WHAT ARE YOUR MOST POPULAR BEERS?**
Racer 5 IPA, Double Aught, Hop Shovel.

**WHICH BEERS ARE YOU PROUDEST OF?**
Our first beer, Ricardo's Red Rocket Ale, is the beer that started it all.

**HAVE ANY OF YOUR BEERS WON AWARDS?**
As of early 2018, Bear Republic had won 25 GABF awards. Additionally, we have won various medals from the World Beer Cup, the Good Food Awards, the Cal. State Fair, and many more.

**WHAT ARE THE BIGGEST CHALLENGES YOUR BREWERY HAS FACED?**
Growth challenges when our city was going through a drought.

**WHAT'S THE ATMOSPHERE LIKE?**
A relaxed, casual dining experience is what you should expect

**INDEPENDENT FAMILY BREWERS**

on your visit. Our pub is a fun, unique departure from a tour of wine country.

We were founded by third- and fourth-generation Sonoma County residents. ✳

### ARE YOU DOG & FAMILY FRIENDLY?

Our brewpubs are family and kid friendly. Dogs are welcome at our Healdsburg brewpub; service dogs only in Rohnert Park.

### DO YOU HAVE FOOD?

We have pub fare such as burgers, pizza, sandwiches, and salads.

### WHAT ELSE CAN YOU TELL US?

Home of the award-winning Racer 5 IPA.

# MAD FRITZ

1282B Vidovich Ave., St. Helena, CA 94574
707-968-5097 • madfritz.com

Tues.–Sun. noon–7 pm.

**WHEN DID YOU OPEN?**

July 2014.

**WHAT ARE YOUR MOST POPULAR BEERS?**

Imperial Rye Stout, Wine Grape Ale, and Golden Strong Ale.

**WHICH BEERS ARE YOU PROUDEST OF?**

Farmers Ale: we have our own malthouse, so we grow, malt, and brew this beer.

**WHAT ARE THE BIGGEST CHALLENGES YOUR BREWERY HAS FACED?**

Growing and malting barley. All our beers are barrel aged, bottled unfiltered, and unfined and naturally carbonated; thus there is a lot of finesse in getting the beers just right.

**WHAT'S THE ATMOSPHERE LIKE?**

A small, intimate tasting experience that offers a unique and educational perspective to the original approach we use to make our beers.

**DO YOU HAVE FOOD?**

No.

**WHAT ELSE CAN YOU TELL US?**

All our beers are named after Aesop's fables, and we offer an amusing interpretation of them on the back label, as well as the origins of all the ingredients in the beers, down to the water sourcing. ❋

# MOONLIGHT BREWING CO.

3350-A Coffey Lane, Santa Rosa, CA 95403
707-528-2537 • moonlightbrewing.com

Fri. 4–8 pm;
Sat. & Sun. 2–8 pm

**WHEN DID YOU OPEN?**
August 1992.

**WHAT ARE YOUR MOST POPULAR BEERS?**
Our (San Francisco–style) Death & Taxes Black Lager and our Reality Czeck-style Pils.

**WHICH BEERS ARE YOU PROUDEST OF?**
All our beers are delicious. Perhaps I might say I am most proud of our herbal (unhopped) beers, since these styles are rare.

**HAVE ANY OF YOUR BEERS WON AWARDS?**
We don't really care about awards. The beer itself is our goal.

**WHAT ARE THE BIGGEST CHALLENGES YOUR BREWERY HAS FACED?**
Surviving 25 years in an ever-changing environment.

**WHAT'S THE ATMOSPHERE LIKE?**
Our tasting room is casual and eclectic. I suppose our brewery is also.

**ARE YOU DOG & FAMILY FRIENDLY?**
Family friendly.

**DO YOU HAVE FOOD?**
Popcorn.

**WHAT ELSE CAN YOU TELL US?**
We are an abbey brewery, the first in the U.S.

We were a single-person operation for about 10 years.

We are not all about the over-use of hops. ✳

# FOGBELT BREWING CO.

1305 Cleveland Ave., Santa Rosa, CA 95401
707-978-3400 • fogbeltbrewing.com

Mon.-Thurs. noon-10 pm; Fri. 11 am-11 pm;
Sat. 11 am-11 pm; Sun. 11 am-10 pm

**WHEN DID YOU OPEN?**
February 2014.

**WHAT ARE YOUR MOST POPULAR BEERS?**
Del Norte IPA, Hyperion Red Ale, Screaming Giant DIPA, Atlas Blonde.

**WHICH BEERS ARE YOU PROUDEST OF?**
Our Atlas Blonde is what we are most proud of because technically it is difficult to brew consistently well. Wet-hop beers are a focus—we work with local hop producers and take from our own hop yard to produce amazingly fresh beer.

**HAVE ANY OF YOUR BEERS WON AWARDS?**
Zephyr Apricot Gose, first place, Cal. State Fair Beer Competition.

**WHAT ARE THE BIGGEST CHALLENGES YOUR BREWERY HAS FACED?**
Growth in a competitive market has been both exciting and challenging, along with our own hurdles of production space in a small brewery.

**WHAT'S THE ATMOSPHERE LIKE?**
Fogbelt has a comfortable and laid-back environment. We focus on fresh and clean beers and strive to make almost everything in-house for our food menu.

The fogbelt is the fog that sits in the redwood trees from the central coast of California up to the Oregon border; because of this, we name all our beers after redwood trees. ❋

### DO YOU HAVE FOOD?

We have a full kitchen and serve a gastropub-style menu with unique items like pretzel bites and zucchini cakes. We make almost everything in-house and have a garden where we grow our own vegetables.

### WHAT ELSE CAN YOU TELL US?

We have our own hop yard for our beer and a garden for our kitchen in our neighboring city Healdsburg.

# RUSSIAN RIVER BREWING CO.

725 4th St., Santa Rosa, CA 95404
707-545-2337 • russianriverbrewing.com

Daily 11 am-midnight

**WHEN DID YOU OPEN?**

1997; reopened in 2004.

**WHAT ARE YOUR MOST POPULAR BEERS?**

Pliny the Elder, Pliny the Younger, Blind Pig, Consecration, STS Pilsner.

**WHICH BEERS ARE YOU PROUDEST OF?**

Whichever one is in my hand at the moment.

**HAVE ANY OF YOUR BEERS WON AWARDS?**

Please see our website for a semicomplete list. We have won the Brewery and Brewmaster of the Year awards at both the GABF and the World Beer Cup for winning the most awards for our beers. Our double IPA, Pliny the Elder, was named Best Beer in America 2009–2016 by the American Homebrewers Association's magazine *Zurmurgy*. Owners Natalie and Vinnie were given the prestigious Brewer's Association Recognition Award at the National Craft Brewers Conference in 2017.

**WHAT ARE THE BIGGEST CHALLENGES YOUR BREWERY HAS FACED?**

Managing the increase in demand while brewing at full capacity for the past several years. Also, providing the best customer experience possible at our brewpub, particularly at very busy times.

**WHAT'S THE ATMOSPHERE LIKE?**

It is a comfortable, casual, pub atmosphere, family friendly, with great food and beer. Our favorite phrase is when people say that RRBC is a world-class brewery!

**ARE YOU DOG & FAMILY FRIENDLY?**

Family friendly.

**DO YOU HAVE FOOD?**

Beer bites are everyone's favorite;

we've been told we have the best pizza in town. We also have wings, calzone, sandwiches, salads, and a couple of appetizer plates.

**WHAT ELSE CAN YOU TELL US?**
We had visitors from nearly every single state and from over 40 different countries during our two-week release of Pliny the Younger in 2017. On any given day, you can walk through our pub and find people from out of state and out of the country visiting RRBC for the first time.

In 2016, the Sonoma County Economic Development Board conducted its second study on our annual Pliny the Younger release. It determined the economic impact on Sonoma County was just under $5 million. That makes us very proud. We're honored to contribute so much economic stimulus to our county and state. ❉

# THIRD STREET ALEWORKS

610 Third St., Santa Rosa, CA 95404
707-523-3060 • thirdstreetaleworks.com

Daily 11:30 am–midnight

**WHEN DID YOU OPEN?**
March 1996.

**WHAT ARE YOUR MOST POPULAR BEERS?**
Puddle Jumper Pale Ale, Bombay Rouge, Bodega Head IPA, Keep Calm & Saison, and Helles Lager.

**WHICH BEERS ARE YOU PROUDEST OF?**
Puddle Jumper is a fantastic beer in its own right, showcasing the wonderful aromatics of Simcoe hops. And we also use the beer (minus Simcoe) as a base for most of our single-hop series beers.

**HAVE ANY OF YOUR BEERS WON AWARDS?**
We have won more than a dozen medals from the Great American Beer Festival and almost as many from the World Beer Cup.

**WHAT ARE THE BIGGEST CHALLENGES YOUR BREWERY HAS FACED?**
Always changing with the times.

**WHAT'S THE ATMOSPHERE LIKE?**
Casual, fun.

**ARE YOU DOG & FAMILY FRIENDLY?**
Dog friendly on patio. Very kid friendly.

**Do you have food?**

Big menu, very eclectic.

**What else?**

The most interesting and unique thing about Third Street Aleworks is that we do not have a flagship list of beers—our beer board changes every day and it evolves over time. It's Darwinian —the beers that people like the most win out over time and the beers that we were making 1, 5, 10, or even 20 years ago are still up on that board regularly only because they stand the test of time. Blarney Sisters Dry Irish Stout, for example, has been brewed essentially unchanged for 20 years—in addition to a loyal local following, that beer has won more critical acclaim and awards than any other dry Irish stout that does not begin with the letter "G." ❄

# HENHOUSE BREWING CO.

322 Bellevue Ave., Santa Rosa, CA 95407
707-978-4577 • henhousebrewing.com

Mon.–Fri. 4–11 pm;
Sat. & Sun. 11 am–9 pm

**WHEN DID YOU OPEN?**

Our first sale was January 24, 2012; the tasting room in Santa Rosa opened in March 2016.

**WHAT ARE YOUR MOST POPULAR BEERS?**

Saison, Honest Day's Work Red Rye Saison, Oyster Stout, and HenHouse IPA.

**WHICH BEERS ARE YOU PROUDEST OF?**

Saison, Honest Day's Work Red Rye Saison, Oyster Stout, and Henhouse IPA. These are all well-balanced, thoughtfully constructed, accessible beers that can delight a variety of palates and pair beautifully with many different dishes.

**HAVE ANY OF YOUR BEERS WON AWARDS?**

Our Belgian-style golden ale took a gold medal at the Cal. State Fair.

**WHAT ARE THE BIGGEST CHALLENGES YOUR BREWERY HAS FACED?**

Constant improvement is the constant challenge. How do we make better beer tomorrow? That's the challenge we try to rise to every day. It has been a challenge to grow our business in a rapid but sustainable manner that allows us to retain our focus on what we have set out to do—produce high-quality craft beer that is taken care of from tank to glass. We look forward to continuing the development of this business that provides Northern California with fresh, cold, delicious craft beer.

At HenHouse, we are stoked to be part of this flourishing craft beer industry, and our fans embody this stoked attitude with their support and enjoyment of our tasty beverages.

## WHAT'S THE ATMOSPHERE LIKE?

The brewery has a relaxed, family-friendly atmosphere where our beer-tenders can often be heard enthusiastically explaining the "hows," "whats," and "whys" of the beers we make to our guests. We love the phrase "Beers you can think about but don't have to."

## DO YOU HAVE FOOD?

We don't have a kitchen, but we partner with the Red Horse Pizza food truck Thursday through Sunday, and we're experimenting with other food trucks in the early part of the week. Outside food is always welcome.

## WHAT ELSE CAN YOU TELL US?

We are HenHouse Brewing Company because our three owners are all natives of Petaluma, CA, the former chicken capital of the world and birthplace of the chicken incubator. Our original two-barrel brewing system was located in a former egg processing facility. ❋

# East Bay

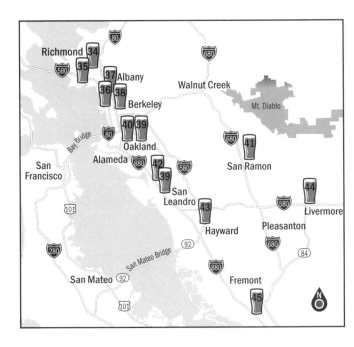

**34.** Benoit Casper Brewing Co., Richmond

**35.** East Brother Beer Co., Richmond

**36.** Ocean View Brew Works, Albany

**37.** Gilman Brewing Co., Berkeley

**38.** Triple Rock Brewing & Alehouse, Berkeley

**39.** Drake's Brewing Co., Oakland

**39.** Drake's Brewing Co., San Leandro

**40.** Federation Brewing, Oakland

**41.** Schubros Brewery, San Ramon

**42.** Cleophus Quealy Beer Co., San Leandro

**43.** Buffalo Bill's Brewery, Hayward

**44.** 8 Bridges Brewing Co., Livermore

**45.** DasBrew, Fremont

# BENOIT CASPER BREWING CO.

1201 Pennsylvania Ave., Richmond, CA 94801
408-695-3449 • bcbrewing.com

Fri. 3–7 pm;
Sat. & Sun. noon–7 pm

**WHEN DID YOU OPEN?**

We were founded in 2014; the taproom opened in January 2015.

**WHAT ARE YOUR MOST POPULAR BEERS?**

Saison de Casper and Pt. Richmond Pale Ale.

**HAVE ANY OF YOUR BEERS WON AWARDS?**

Vienna Lager, gold at 2017 Cal. State Fair; Pt. Richmond Pale Ale, silver at 2015 Cal. State Fair; Pils-4-Rils, bronze at 2016 Cal. State Fair; Saison de Casper, gold at 2016 Best of Craft Beer Awards; ALTen Amber, gold at 2017 NorCal Brew Competition.

**WHAT ARE THE BIGGEST CHALLENGES YOUR BREWERY HAS FACED?**

Making enough beer! We run

a small brewhouse, 3.5 barrels, and we brew up to eight times per week to keep up with demand. Being small and boot-strapped, we are forced to grow organically in small, calculated steps. Our location is off the beaten path and in an industrial warehouse, so we rely on social media and word of mouth to draw customers into our taproom.

### What's the atmosphere like?

Benoit-Casper is nestled in a warehouse space that we've converted into a brewery/taproom. Descriptions from some of our customers: "Very different beers and a cool environment." "Hidden gem." "This small-town brewery is destined to grow, and I really believe that they will be expanding once everyone catches onto how good they are." "Off the hook, most random place in Richmond!"

### Are you dog & family friendly?

Yes and yes.

### Do you have food?

We do not serve food, but we do provide complimentary popcorn and host barbecues, local food trucks, and vendors on a regular basis.

### What else can you tell us?

We are Richmond's first brewery. ❊

# EAST BROTHER BEER CO.

1001 Canal Blvd., #C-2, Richmond, CA 94804
510-230-4081 • eastbrotherbeer.com

Wed. & Thurs. 4-8 pm; Fri. 4-9pm;
Sat. noon-9 pm; Sun. noon-8 pm

**WHEN DID YOU OPEN?**
December 2016.

**WHAT ARE YOUR MOST POPULAR BEERS?**
Red Lager and Red IPA.

**WHICH BEERS ARE YOU PROUDEST OF?**
We're particularly fond of our Bo Pils (Czech-style pilsner) and our Oatmeal Stout. Both of these beers require a nuanced touch in getting the right balance (of hops and malt for the Bo Pils, and dry and sweet for the Oatmeal Stout), and we're very happy with the balance we've achieved with both of these beers.

**WHAT ARE THE BIGGEST CHALLENGES YOUR BREWERY HAS FACED?**
Financing the purchase and buildout of the brewery—we've done it with SBA loans and with funds we've saved—and keeping up with demand. After being open for only a couple of months, we realized we'd need to expand, and we added a concrete pad and (bigger) fermenters six months later.

**WHAT'S THE ATMOSPHERE LIKE?**
We established our brewery in an industrial section of Richmond, a city with a rich industrial history, and the beers we are making reflect this hard-earned heritage. We make classic styles—from pilsners to stouts to IPAs—and aim for all of them to be balanced, clean-finishing, easy-drinking beers. Our brand reflects this minimalist, unassuming nature, as does our taproom, which is populated by a very diverse crowd from our immediate and surrounding communities, the composition of which reflects a broad cross-

section of ages and ethnicities. Our taproom has become known as a comfortable, welcoming place to chill with friends and family (and kids and dogs) and to play a game of Ping-Pong or a round of cornhole.

**ARE YOU DOG & FAMILY FRIENDLY?**

Yes and yes.

**DO YOU HAVE FOOD?**

We have a rotating set of food trucks every day that we're open—choices range from barbecue to pizza to burgers to pasta.

**WHAT ELSE CAN YOU TELL US?**

Our name—East Brother—comes from a lighthouse located in the San Pablo Bay (the north-ern part of San Francisco Bay) that's been continuously operating for almost 150 years; the funny thing is that hardly anyone in the Bay Area has heard of it, with the exception of people who live or were raised in Richmond.

Despite the industrial nature of our location, our taproom is located right next to a regional park marsh. You can listen to a massive chorus of frogs in the winter and wild turkeys gobbling in the summer.

Our taproom is very dog friendly, so one of the leading themes we see posted on social media about us is pictures of people's dogs taking a nap on our cool concrete after a long walk! ❄

# OCEAN VIEW BREW WORKS

625 San Pablo Ave., Albany, CA 94706
510-280-5127 • oceanviewbrews.com

Tues.–Fri. 3-9 pm;
Sat. & Sun. noon–8 pm

**WHEN DID YOU OPEN?**

February 2018.

**WHAT ARE YOUR MOST POPULAR BEERS?**

We rotate our beers frequently, so there isn't one particular best seller. Our IPAs are always enjoyed, and our English-style beers are spot on. We try to keep a balanced beer menu that also offers something new and different like a slightly sour beer with a fruity component.

**WHICH OF YOUR BEERS ARE YOU PROUDEST OF, AND WHY?**

Admiral Simcoe. This was the first beer we brewed on our professional system, and it was made entirely with Admiral malts (the only malting house in California). This well-balanced session IPA was very well received. The malts are all from the California Central Valley; we are really excited to brew many more locally sourced beers!

**HAVE ANY OF YOUR BEERS WON AWARDS?**

Both our brewers have won many awards in the homebrewing community. We have not yet entered into any competitions.

**WHAT ARE THE BIGGEST CHALLENGES YOUR BREWERY HAS FACED?**

This was a completely self-funded operation; we opened when our kids were one and three years old. Much of the work was done by ourselves and our families, which definitely impacted our timeline. We have a finite amount of interior square footage, and we struggled to meet all code requirements and maintain as much taproom seating as possible. In the end, we were able to create a warm and inviting space in less than a year!

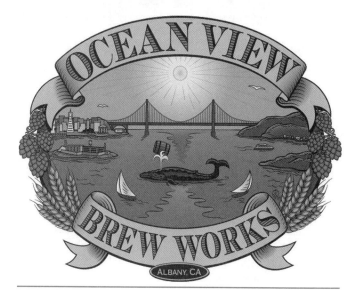

OCEAN VIEW

BREW WORKS

ALBANY, CA

### What's the atmosphere like?

Ocean View Brew Works has a very nice flow between the indoor and outdoor spaces. It is a small taproom with a larger beer garden. There are many small details, such as a one-of-a-kind bar top and custom doors, that add character. We wanted to blend the industrial feel of a brewery with vintage and specially crafted elements to create a unique ambiance.

### Is your brewery dog & family friendly?

*Very*! Our goal was to provide the space we searched for with our dog and kids. We have game board table tops, oversized games in the beer garden, and a Lego table! More elements are in the works to entertain little ones so the adults can enjoy our craft!

### Do you have food?

We have rotating food pop-ups that feature local chefs and their delicious offerings.

### What else can you tell us?

Almost everyone involved in the process of creating this brewery and taproom is a family member or close friend. Ocean View is a showcase of artistic talents that complement the delicious beer! ✳

# GILMAN BREWING CO.

912 Gilman St., Berkeley, CA 94710
510-556-8701 • gilmanbrew.com

Sun.-Thurs. noon-10 pm;
Fri. & Sat. noon-11 pm

**WHEN DID YOU OPEN?**
2016.

**WHAT ARE YOUR MOST POPULAR BEERS?**
Saisons, IPAs, and double IPAs.

**WHICH BEERS ARE YOU PROUDEST OF?**
All our saisons—we do them right. We take the time to get them fully attenuated, nice, and dry, as they should be! The complexity you can produce in this style using just the tradi-tional four ingredients—malted barley, yeast, hops, and water—is amazing.

**HAVE ANY OF YOUR BEERS WON AWARDS?**
After being open only six months, we won two gold medals in the LA International Commercial Beer Competition for our Maison de Campagne, a French-style saison, and our Ferme Noire, a dark saison

brewed with Brettanomyces. Two months later, we won three silver medals in the NorCal Brew Commercial competition at the Sonoma State Fair for our Ferme Noire (again), our Champ Rochaux (a nectarine saison), and our Smoked Porter.

**WHAT ARE THE BIGGEST CHALLENGES YOUR BREWERY HAS FACED?**

City of Berkeley building/zoning delays for construction and a year-long delay for our federal TTB license.

**WHAT'S THE ATMOSPHERE LIKE?**

Industrial, comfortable, retro, friendly, unique.

**ARE YOU DOG & FAMILY FRIENDLY?**

Yes to both.

**DO YOU HAVE FOOD?**

Snacks and food trucks or caterers on some days—check the website!

**WHAT ELSE CAN YOU TELL US?**

Almost everything in the brewery was fabricated here. We have an old anvil we use to make hooks, shelving, etc. We design and fabricate our own flight holders, tap handles, light fixtures, and much of the furniture in-house.

The owner/brewers/general manager installed the entire brewery themselves.

The building was home for years to the Autoshop. The ghost of the Autoshop (a squirrel named Steve) roams the place at night, wreaking havoc on equipment, opening valves, and messing up neatly arranged lines of machinery. ❈

# TRIPLE ROCK
## BREWING & ALEHOUSE

1920 Shattuck Ave., Berkeley, CA 94707
510-843-2739 • triplerock.com

Open daily at 11:30

**WHEN DID YOU OPEN?**

1986, making us the fifth brew-pub in the United States and the only one currently operated by the original owners (and we're still using the original equipment!).

**WHAT ARE YOUR MOST POPULAR BEERS?**

We are best known for our IPAXs, our West Coast IPAs, and our Monkey Head Arboreal Ale, but customers look forward to exciting and innovative brews anytime they drink with us.

**WHICH BEERS ARE YOU PROUDEST OF?**

I'm proudest of the constant revolving one-off beers we brew—everything from unique Belgians and single-hop beers to stouts and porters and barrel-aged beers. But if I had to pick one, it would be the 30th Anniversary Barrel Aged Black Rock Porter.

It's very cool to be involved in such a milestone.

**HAVE ANY OF YOUR BEERS WON AWARDS?**

7-Fifty, 2010 GABF bronze; Collaborative Evil, 2010 GABF silver; Puddy Porter, 2011 GABF bronze; Red Rock, 2013 GABF bronze, 2010 GABF bronze, 2010 World Beer Cup silver, 2009 GABF silver; Rye Smile, 2013 GABF silver; Tropical Stout, 2017 Cal. State Fair silver.

**WHAT ARE THE BIGGEST CHALLENGES YOUR BREWERY HAS FACED?**

At the time John and Reid Martin established Triple Rock, many local and state laws prohibited the retail sale of beer on-site. The brothers were repeatedly advised to abandon their chosen site and to locate their brewery in the industrial area of Berkeley. At the time, city bureaucrats had never heard of a "brewpub" and there was neighborhood concern about a "factory" being allowed to operate in downtown Berkeley. Finally, after a year and a half, they received the seven variances necessary from the city of Berkeley zoning codes and were able to commence construction.

Triple Rock faces the same challenges other small breweries face in that we need to be constantly listening to the voices of independent craft beer drinkers and give them what they want.

### What's the atmosphere like?

Triple Rock oozes timeless American tavern and dive bar vibes, while our recent expansion offers customers a taste of the modern. Our guests come from every aspect of the Berkeley community. Students and professors alike head to our alehouse for brews and bar food, mingling with Berkeley natives who've been drinking with us since the beginning. On any given day, you can chat with regulars who have decades of Triple Rock stories sitting next to amateur craft beer drinkers who are just starting to dip their toes into the industry.

### Do you have food?

Our buffalo wings are a must for any carnivore, and our marinated mushroom wrap and black rock BBQ seitan are filling options for those who don't eat meat.

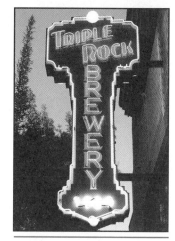

Our burgers are a special blend of responsibly raised, dry-aged beef provided exclusively for us from Cream Co. Meat, and our Beer Can Chicken is free range.

### What else can you tell us?

Thursdays are known as Monkey Head Night, the only day of the week where guests can enjoy Monkey Head Arboreal Ale. This brew has garnered a cult following, something of a rite of passage in the Cal Berkeley community, and you can expect a line to get in halfway around the block on any given Thursday.

Triple Rock originally opened under the name Roaring Rock Brewery. The name change was the result of a legal battle with Rolling Rock Brewing. A couple of rejected names: Foamy Rock and Rolling Duck. ✻

# DRAKE'S BREWING CO.

Barrel House: 1933 Davis St., San Leandro, CA 94577
Dealership: 2325 Broadway Auto Rd., Oakland, CA 94612
510-568-2739 • drinkdrakes.com

Check website for hours

### WHEN DID YOU OPEN?

Opened by Roger Lind in 1989 and purchased by John Martin and Roy Kirkorian in 2008.

### WHAT ARE YOUR MOST POPULAR BEERS?

Our best-selling beers are Best Coast IPA, 1500 Pale Ale, and Denogginizer Double IPA. We are fortunate to have three strong, viable flagship brands that are all continuing to grow in the double digits.

### WHICH ARE YOUR FAVORITE BEERS?

It's hard to pick a favorite child, and these beers are like our children. The answer would change depending on who you talk to and which day of the week it is. At the moment, we are particularly thrilled with the Aroma Coma 2xIPA recipe as well as our limited-release Foraging Raccoon IPA.

### HAVE ANY OF YOUR BEERS WON AWARDS?

Most of our mainline beers have won awards, but our consistently top-awarded beers are 1500 Pale Ale (Cal. State Beer Competition), Rye Robustito (GABF silver/World Beer Cup bronze), and Black Robusto (GABF silver).

### WHAT ARE THE BIGGEST CHALLENGES YOUR BREWERY HAS FACED?

The biggest challenge we've faced over the past few years is expanding to keep up with the demand of continued growth. Yeah, it's a "good problem," but we have to walk the razor's edge making sure we keep both our taps and the trucks filled. We've quadrupled the brewery's capacity over the past couple of years without having any significant downtime (and we're often brewing 24 hours a day). We've also had the engineering challenges of building a brewery that runs among six separate buildings, none of which were large enough to house production independently.

Our brewery is gritty rather than pretty. We embrace that edgy, other-side-of-the-tracks vibe, where our facility lives in a 1940s Dodge plant.

The Dealership is dog friendly in the outdoor garden.

Drake's Barrel House has an on-site kitchen serving burgers, salads, sandwiches, tater tots, and other snacks adjacent to the brewery. Food is served out of the Duck Truck Food Kitchen outside of the taproom. The Dealership has a full kitchen.

We often call ourselves the "longest" brewery on the West Coast; our beer runs through overhead steel pipes over 200 yards from the brewhouse to bright tanks in three different buildings.

Drake's was originally a subtle nod to Sir Francis Drake; however, in 2008 we fully embraced a left turn toward embracing our love of all things mallard.

Denogginizer, one of our three best-selling beers, is an obscure Seinfeld reference about a serial killer loose in Central Park who was relieving victims of their

heads. However, it was first used at Drake's when one of our brewers almost got "denogginized" by an over-pressurized tank that held an as-yet-unnamed double IPA. ✳

40

# FEDERATION BREWING

420 3rd St., Oakland, CA 94607
510-496-4228 • federationbrewing.com

Wed. & Thurs. 4-9 pm; Fri. 4-midnight;
Sat. noon-midnight; Sun. noon-9 pm

**WHEN DID YOU OPEN?**

Established 2014; tasting room opened March 2017.

**WHAT ARE YOUR MOST POPULAR BEERS?**

In the Weeds IPA, Behind You! Blonde Ale, Ceremony Saison.

**WHICH BEERS ARE YOU PROUDEST OF?**

I am proud of all our beers, but the Ceremony Saison holds a special place in my heart as it was first designed as a champagne toast substitute for my wedding in 2015.

**WHAT ARE THE BIGGEST CHALLENGES YOUR BREWERY HAS FACED?**

The same challenges any small business faces, but we have a growing team to help us find our way. That's why we call ourselves a federation: we have a collaborative work environment that draws inspiration from every-thing/everyone around us. Our community is our most valuable asset.

**WHAT'S THE ATMOSPHERE LIKE?**

Chill vibe, creative, inclusive, and unique.

**DO YOU HAVE FOOD?**

We host local food vendors on a regular basis.

**WHAT ELSE CAN YOU TELL US?**

The founders met in middle school band. We named a number of our beers after silly

service industry terms, such as "In the Weeds," "Low Boy," and "Behind You!" We used to be called Champion Brewing, but that was before we knew about trademarks. ✳

# SCHUBROS BREWERY

12893 Alcosta Blvd., Suite N, San Ramon, CA 94583
510-999-6593 • schubrosbrewery.com

Thurs. & Fri. 4–9 pm;
Sat. 2–7 pm

**WHEN DID YOU OPEN?**

2012.

**WHAT ARE YOUR MOST POPULAR BEERS?**

680 Mahogany, Las Trampas Pale Ale, and Ship to Shore beers—a rotating line of pales and IPAs.

**WHICH BEERS ARE YOU PROUDEST OF?**

Inverness, a bourbon barrel-aged, Scottish wee heavy. This was our best beer in my opinion. We nailed it—perfect for the style, with a wonderful complexity brought in by the barrel aging.

**WHAT ARE THE BIGGEST CHALLENGES YOUR BREWERY HAS FACED?**

The landlord.

**WHAT'S THE ATMOSPHERE LIKE?**

Small, hidden, industrial.

**ARE YOU DOG & FAMILY FRIENDLY?**

Yes and yes.

**DO YOU HAVE FOOD?**

Peanuts and pretzels only—but we encourage ordering food.

**WHAT ELSE CAN YOU TELL US?**

Our wall design has become famous: 6,400 end cuts of wood. Hand cut, hand sanded, hand affixed. It delayed our opening by three weeks.

Handicap accessible.

We aren't allowed any signage, so allot/allow yourself a few extra minutes to find us. It will be worth it! ❈

# CLEOPHUS QUEALY BEER CO.

448 Hester St., San Leandro, CA 94577
510-463-4534 • cleoph.us

Thurs. & Fri. 3-9 pm;
Sat. noon-8 pm

**WHEN DID YOU OPEN?**
December 2014.

**WHAT ARE YOUR MOST POPULAR BEERS?**
We do very small batches and experiment with ingredients and flavors, so our tap list changes frequently—this means that our most popular beers change pretty often. Belgian-style beers are popular, and we also do a lot of barrel-aged beers with fruit that are a hit with newcomers to our tasting room and regulars alike. Over the past couple of years, we've found that our rye pale ale and our dry-hopped saison have been favorites, so we tend to have at least one of those on tap year-round.

**WHICH BEERS ARE YOU PROUDEST OF?**
We make a barrel-aged quadrupel with vanilla and orange peel in the winter that people get very excited about and a barrel-aged golden ale with raspberries called Framboos in the summer. Neither are exactly what people expect; many people equate quadrupels with sweetness, but ours is rich and balanced without all the sugar. And Framboos isn't the same as the sour-style framboise—it's dry, more like a white wine than a sour beer. Both are just lovely, and even people who don't like beer tend to love them.

**HAVE ANY OF YOUR BEERS WON AWARDS?**
Not yet, but Dan and Peter—our founders—took home quite a few homebrew awards before opening Cleophus Quealy.

**WHAT ARE THE BIGGEST CHALLENGES YOUR BREWERY HAS FACED?**
The toughest part has been letting people know that we're

here. We're something of a hidden gem, especially since we're off the beaten path a bit, in an industrial area of San Leandro. We definitely aren't in a spot that gets any foot traffic, so we have to work all the harder to let people know we exist. But word is slowly getting out, especially with Drake's and 21st Amendment down the road, and people are realizing that San Leandro is great for beer-centric adventures.

### What's the atmosphere like?

"Cozy" is the description we hear the most. We're small, which makes our tasting room feel homey and intimate, and though we're in a warehouse, we try to make it feel inviting and homelike. We have reclaimed wood on the walls, which warms up the brewery and takes that impersonal, industrial edge off. And we don't have any walls between the tasting room and the brewery—the only thing dividing the space is our barrels. People can see and sit alongside the barrels we're using to age beers, and we like having such an important part of our beer-making process so visible.

### Do you have food?

We have a partnership with a fantastic food truck, Canasta Kitchen.

Their street tacos and nachos are just amazing, and they make fish tacos that are just ridiculously delicious. They're also kind enough to indulge us by making fish and chips with the same crispy cod fillets they use in fish tacos, served with garlic fries. It's great beer food.

### What else can you tell us?

The question we hear most is, "What does your name mean?" followed by, "How do you pronounce it?" Our name is a nod to Dan's and Peter's family histories—Dan had a great-great-great-grandfather named Cleophus, and Peter's mom's maiden name is Quealy. Our beers are inspired by old beer styles and brewing traditions, so it was only fitting that our name would reflect this old-world inspiration. As for how it's pronounced ... Well, it gets easier to say after a beer or two. Trust us. ❋

# BUFFALO BILL'S BREWERY

1082 B St., Hayward, CA 94541
510-886-9823 • buffalobillsbrewery.com

Sun.-Thurs. 11 am-8:45 pm;
Fri. & Sat. 11 am-11:45 pm

**WHEN DID YOU OPEN?**
1983.

**WHAT ARE YOUR MOST POPULAR BEERS?**
Tasmanian Devil, Alimony IPA, America's Original Pumpkin Ale, and Blood Orange Imperial Ale.

**WHICH BEERS ARE YOU PROUDEST OF?**
America's Original Pumpkin Ale, Tasmanian Devil, and Alimony IPA because these were all the first in their category in America.

**HAVE ANY OF YOUR BEERS WON AWARDS?**
Best of Craft Beer Awards: Winter Ale (gold), Pumpkin Ale (bronze). Other beers that have won awards: Blueberry Oatmeal Stout, Strawberry Doppel, Blood Orange, Orange Blossom Cream Ale, Strawberry Blonde Ale.

**WHAT ARE THE BIGGEST CHALLENGES YOUR BREWERY HAS FACED?**
Access to market and high taxes.

**WHAT'S THE ATMOSPHERE LIKE?**
Casual atmosphere; warm and vibrant; quality pub fare.

**ARE YOU DOG & FAMILY FRIENDLY?**
Family friendly.

**DO YOU HAVE FOOD?**
We serve lunch and dinner,

the same menu for both. It is a casual menu emphasizing quality burgers, pizzas, sandwiches, and salads, as well as a variety of appetizers, including nachos, calamari, a hummus plate, and our locally renowned poppers.

**WHAT ELSE CAN YOU TELL US?**

Buffalo Bill's is one of America's first brewpubs.

We helped launch what has been coined "the craft beer renaissance."

We were originally owned by world-renowned photographer Bill Owens.

A sidewalk sign that was used in front of Buffalo Bill's Brewery beginning in 1983 is now at the Smithsonian American History Museum (along with other beloved objects from the early days of BBB) for inclusion in their American Brewing History Initiative. ✻

# 8 BRIDGES BREWING CO.

332 Earhart Way, Livermore, CA 94566
925-961-9160 • eightbridgesbrewing.com

Wed. & Thurs. 4–8 pm; Fri. noon–10 pm;
Sat. noon–11 pm; Sun. noon–6 pm

**WHEN DID YOU OPEN?**
February 2014.

**WHAT ARE YOUR MOST POPULAR BEERS?**
Twisted Red, a red ale; Golden Nektar, a German pilsner; O'Beardsley's Stout; Silenus the Dude, a Belgian IPA; Ananas-anator, a double IPA; Wit from Tangier, a Belgian wit.

**WHICH BEERS ARE YOU PROUDEST OF?**
They're all our babies so it's hard to pick one, but brewmaster Justin is currently most proud of the Wit from Tangier because it embodies all the goals he had for the beer.

**HAVE ANY OF YOUR BEERS WON AWARDS?**
O'Beardsley's Stout, Twisted Red, Golden Nektar, Das Mutt Kolsch.

**WHAT ARE THE BIGGEST CHALLENGES YOUR BREWERY HAS FACED?**
Adding team members.

**WHAT'S THE ATMOSPHERE LIKE?**
People come in with the expectation of enjoying one or two of our beers but end up telling us that "there isn't one we didn't like." It's a friendly, comfortable, and warm environment—"You have the personal

touch that brings me back to Eight Bridges."

**ARE YOU DOG & FAMILY FRIENDLY?**

Dog friendly and family friendly.

**DO YOU HAVE FOOD?**

We offer snacks, including beef jerky made with our beer. Our customers have learned that they can have a lot more fun bringing in the food they want or stopping along the way to pick up exactly what they want.

**WHAT ELSE CAN YOU TELL US?**

We've had a full wedding in the brewery.

We make a beer annually, using the hops (California Cluster) grown historically and currently in Pleasanton, CA. ❀

# DASBREW

44356 South Grimmer Blvd., Fremont, CA 94538
510-270-5345 • dasbrewinc.com

Mon.-Thurs. 4:30-9 pm; Fri. 4:30-10 pm;
Sat. & Sun. 2-9 pm

**WHEN DID YOU OPEN?**
DasBrew opened in 2010; the tasting room opened in 2013.

**WHAT ARE YOUR MOST POPULAR BEERS?**
Mean Monkey Hefeweizen, Revealing Red Ale, and Buxom Blonde Kolsch.

**WHICH BEERS ARE YOU PROUDEST OF?**
The Mean Monkey Hefeweizen is our flagship beer and has beautiful banana/clove flavors. We import our grains and yeast from Germany to achieve this.

**HAVE ANY OF YOUR BEERS WON AWARDS?**
We won the 2016 bronze medal for Mean Monkey as the best German beer at the San Diego International Beer Festival.

**WHAT ARE THE BIGGEST CHALLENGES YOUR BREWERY HAS FACED?**
Our biggest challenges have been fighting with the city of Fremont, first to open the brewery and then the tasting room, since a small beer manufacturer had never been here before. Once that was accomplished, battles with PG&E began; we wanted to install gas so we could power our 15-barrel system. We've worked out our issues with the city, but PG&E is still a thorn.

**WHAT'S THE ATMOSPHERE LIKE?**
We have a very relaxed, comfortable, and homey atmosphere where people can come and sit indoors or outdoors and enjoy delicious handcrafted beers. We have been described as "Bohemian" with an "underground flair" because we have tables and chairs set up in the parking lot. People love it!

**DO YOU HAVE FOOD?**
We serve DasBites—small snacks such as chips, pickles, soft Bavarian pretzels with mustard or nacho cheese, and beer nuts.

We have catered food on Thursdays and Fridays.

## WHAT ELSE CAN YOU TELL US?

Jan Schutze and Priscilla La Rocca are co-owners of DasBrew. That's why our motto is "German Beers with an American Finish." Jan was born in Hamburg, Germany, and started drinking and brewing beer at age three. His grandmother Pearle was a good teacher, and our Schlager Lager is based on her homebrew recipe. Our pilsner is named after Grandma Pearle.

We used to have a squirrel eating the spent grains, and she got very fat. Then she would beg for mini pretzels from the tasting room customers. We named her Pearle the Squirrel.

Schnapps is our fierce brewery dog, a 13-pound terrier, and the model for our Red Sled Holiday Ale. ✳

# San Francisco and Marin

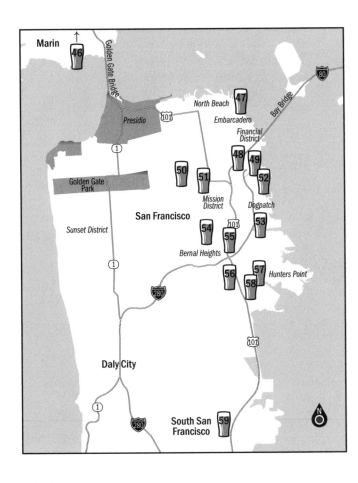

46. State Room Brewery, 1132 4th St., San Rafael

47. Fort Point Beer, San Francisco Ferry Building, San Francisco

48. Thirsty Bear Organic Brewery, 661 Howard St., San Francisco

49. 21st Amendment Brewery, 563 2nd St., San Francisco

50. Black Sands Brewery, 701 Haight St., San Francisco

51. Standard Deviant Brewing, 280 14th St., San Francisco

52. Triple Voodoo Brewery, 2245 3rd St., San Francisco

53. Harmonic Brewing, 1050 26th St., San Francisco

54. Old Bus Tavern, 3193 Mission St., San Francisco

55. Bare Bottle Brew Co., 1525 Cortland Ave., San Francisco

56. Ferment Drink Repeat (FDR), 2636 San Bruno Ave.,
    San Francisco

57. Laughing Monk Brewing, 1439 Egbert Ave., San Francisco

58. Seven Stills Brewery & Distillery, 1439 Egbert Ave.,
    San Francisco

59. Armstrong Brewing Co., 415 Grand Ave, South San Francisco

# STATE ROOM BREWERY

1132 4th St., San Rafael, CA 9490
415-295-7929 • stateroombrewery.com

Tues. & Wed. 11:30 am–10 pm; Thurs.–Sat. 11:30 am–midnight;
Sun. 11:30 am–10 pm

**WHEN DID YOU OPEN?**
January 2016.

**WHAT ARE YOUR MOST POPULAR BEERS?**
Patriot Pilsner, closely followed by Franklin's Tower IPA.

**WHICH BEERS ARE YOU PROUDEST OF?**
Our pilsner—it is based on our brewmaster's recipe from a previous brewery he worked at that won a GABF gold.

**HAVE ANY OF YOUR BEERS WON AWARDS?**
Uncle John's Barleywine won silver in the American Strong Ale category at the Cal. State Fair in 2017.

**WHAT ARE THE BIGGEST CHALLENGES YOUR BREWERY HAS FACED?**
We had a fire in our kitchen and had to close for a few months. Now we are back and better than ever.

**WHAT'S THE ATMOSPHERE LIKE?**
Comfortable, warm, and easy.

**ARE YOU DOG & FAMILY FRIENDLY?**
Family friendly.

**STATE ROOM**
BREWERY · BAR · KITCHEN
NORTH CALIFORNIA

**Do you have food?**
We are a farm-to-table gastropub.

**What else?**
We have skeeball.

All employees wear red shoes.

John Muir is our mascot, and we play his biography audio book in our bathrooms. ✳

THE GREAT SEAL OF THE STATE ROOM

EST. 1769

BREWERY · BAR · KITCHEN

**47**

# FORT POINT BEER

Taproom: San Francisco Ferry Building, One the Embarcadero
San Francisco, CA 94111
415-818-3993 • fortpointbeer.com

Mon.-Fri. 11 am-6 pm;
Sat. 10 am-10 pm; Sun. 11 am-6 pm

**WHEN DID YOU OPEN?**

2014.

**WHAT ARE YOUR MOST POPULAR BEERS?**

KSA, a light and crisp kolsch-style ale, and Villager, a San Francisco–style IPA.

**WHICH BEERS ARE YOU PROUDEST OF?**

Park, a beer that combines many brewing traditions into one refreshing, aromatic package. It includes Belgian Biere de Garge yeast, northwest Citra hops, and German pilsner and pale wheat malts.

**HAVE ANY OF YOUR BEERS WON AWARDS?**

KSA won the Cal. State Fair gold 2015 and bronze 2016; Manzanita won the Cal. State

Fair gold 2015 and Good Food Awards 2014 and 2015; Summer Porter won the GABF silver 2015; Westfalia won the Cal. State Fair Bronze 2016.

**WHAT ARE THE BIGGEST CHALLENGES YOUR BREWERY HAS FACED?**

Growing and scaling a brewery in a densely populated city is always a challenge. Fort Point is not afraid to get creative with space and process to accommodate. Brewing in the Golden Gate National Recreation Area presents some unique challenges as well, for example, abiding by rules and regulations and access during holidays!

**WHAT'S THE ATMOSPHERE LIKE?**

A modern interpretation of a historic, San Francisco place:

friendly, approachable, and well designed.

Yes.

Golden Gate Meat Company hot dogs with Acme buns; Firebrand pretzels.

Fort Point is one of the only breweries nationwide to make beer in a national park (the Presidio in the Golden Gate National Recreation Area).

Fort Point is a self-distributed brewery, serving more than 1,700 accounts (as of mid-2017) through our own logistics network. ❋

**48**

# THIRSTY BEAR ORGANIC BREWERY

661 Howard St., San Francisco, CA 94105
415-974-0905 • thirstybear.com

Mon.–Thurs. 11:30 am–10 pm; Fri. 11:30 am–11 pm;
Sat. noon–11 pm; Sun. noon–10 pm

**WHEN DID YOU OPEN?**
September 1996.

**WHAT ARE YOUR MOST POPULAR BEERS?**
Our Howard Street IPA flies out the door!

**WHICH BEERS ARE YOU PROUDEST OF?**
I enjoy producing what we call our "stave series." A stave is a plank of wood that makes up the body of a barrel. Whenever we age or ferment a beer in a barrel, we call it a "stave series"; for example, Stave Series #21: Fruit Salad soured along with fruit. I prefer to work with local distilleries and wineries when picking up barrels. St. George Spirits, Spirit Works, Sutton Cellars, and Oro en Paz are some producers we have collaborated with.

### Have any of your beers won awards?

Our Black Bear Lager took bronze in the 2004 World Beer Cup for German-style schwarzbier.

### What are the biggest challenges your brewery has faced?

When I started at Thirsty Bear, there were about seven to nine breweries in San Francisco. There are now roughly thirty! We have to be innovative to stay on people's minds.

### What's the atmosphere like?

We are a full-service brewery/restaurant offering creative, certified organic beers, an extensive wine list by the bottle and the tap, and an impressive bar.

### Do you have food?

We serve Spanish tapas coupled with local Californian ingredients.

### What else can you tell us?

We offer flamenco shows every Sunday night.

All the beers are certified organic.

We have been in business for more than 20 years, making us the oldest brewpub in San Francisco! ❋

# 49

# 21ST AMENDMENT BREWERY

Pub: 563 2nd St., San Francisco, CA 94107
415-369-0900 • 21st-amendment.com

Brewery/taproom: 2010 Williams St., San Leandro, CA 94577
510-595-2111 • 21st-amendment.com

Pub: Mon.–Sat. 11:30 am–midnight; Sun. 10:00 am–midnight
Brewery/taproom: Tues.–Thurs. 3–9 pm;
Fri. & Sat. noon–10 pm; Sun. noon–7 pm

**WHAT ARE YOUR MOST POPULAR BEERS?**

Brew Free! Or Die IPA, Hell or High Watermelon Wheat Beer.

**WHICH BEERS ARE YOU PROUDEST OF?**

All of them! Love and attention go into each and every batch we brew.

**HAVE ANY OF YOUR BEERS WON AWARDS?**

Toaster Pastry Double Red won the 2016 World Beer Cup bronze; El Sully Mexican-style Lager won the 2016 Great American Beer Festival gold; Down to Earth Session IPA won the 2016 World Beer Cup silver.

**WHAT ARE THE BIGGEST CHALLENGES YOUR BREWERY HAS FACED?**

Expansion and distribution. Real estate in the Bay Area isn't cheap, so we've always had to balance growth with the cost of expanding our production facilities.

### WHAT'S THE ATMOSPHERE LIKE?

If you love the San Francisco Giants, you'll love our SF pub. Come on game day, but be sure to wear your Giants gear! And if you head to our San Leandro taproom, be sure to bring your four-legged friends.

### ARE YOU DOG & FAMILY FRIENDLY?

Yes and yes. Dogs are welcome in our outdoor patio area.

### DO YOU HAVE FOOD?

Our SF pub serves classic pub food with a California twist. We have food trucks at our San Leandro taproom; we plan to expand and build out a kitchen there.

### WHAT ELSE CAN YOU TELL US?

Our cofounders, Nico Freccia and Shaun O'Sullivan, are both avid homebrewers who continue to brew at home to this day. Nearly all our recipes began as homebrew batches.

Rosie, our small 200-barrel fermenter in San Leandro, is for one-off experimental brews and is named after one of our office pups.

In 2016, we used over one million pounds of fresh watermelon in making our Hell or High Watermelon wheat beer. ❋

# BLACK SANDS BREWERY

701 Haight St., San Francisco, CA 94117
415-534-5194 • blacksandsbeer.com

Tues.-Thurs. 8 am-midnight; Fri. 8 am-1 am;
Sat. 8 am-1 am; Sun. 8 am-midnight

**WHEN DID YOU OPEN?**
July 2015.

**WHAT ARE YOUR MOST POPULAR BEERS?**
Night Song SMASH (single malt and single hop IPA); Exit Paradise Pineapple Saison.

**WHICH BEERS ARE YOU PROUDEST OF?**
Out Baja—a kolsch. It's a style we didn't expect to enter into, but we did a test batch that came out so well that we're brewing it on a regular schedule. As a non-kolsch lover, this beer changed my mind. When you doubt that you can find a kolsch you like, just brew one you do like.

**BLACK SANDS BREWERY**
SAN FRANCISCO, CALIFORNIA

### WHAT ARE THE BIGGEST CHALLENGES YOUR BREWERY HAS FACED?

Keeping up with demand. We've been at 100 percent capacity since day one!

### WHAT'S THE ATMOSPHERE LIKE?

Casual, clean, modern, affordable, open space, transparent, quality food, quality coffee, and, most of all, quality beers.

### ARE YOU DOG & FAMILY FRIENDLY?

Family friendly.

### DO YOU HAVE FOOD?

Elevated bar food and snacks.

We offered the 22nd best burger in America in 2017. We have a rotating seasonal menu—featuring fresh ingredients—from fish tacos to ribs to grain bowls, vegetarian, and vegan options. Our specialties are house-made pickles and beef jerky. There is always something new, and our food is always fresh.

### WHAT ELSE CAN YOU TELL US?

Black Sands was constructed by the four owners, who were all homebrewers. We're 100 percent independently owned. ✳

**51**

# STANDARD DEVIANT BREWING

280 14th St., San Francisco, CA 94103
415-590-2550 • standarddeviantbrewing.com

Wed. 4-9 pm; Thurs. 4-10 pm; Fri. 4-midnight;
Sat. 1 pm-midnight; Sun. 1-9 pm

**WHEN DID YOU OPEN?**
July 2016.

**WHAT ARE YOUR MOST POPULAR BEERS?**
Callista Pale Ale, kolschs, saisons, and IPAs.

**WHICH BEERS ARE YOU PROUDEST OF?**
Callista Pale Ale. It's a single-hopped pale ale that is perfectly balanced. Crisp and refreshing, with great aroma and light malt, this beer is drinkable at any and all times! And it's a very uncommon hop.

**WHAT ARE THE BIGGEST CHALLENGES YOUR BREWERY HAS FACED?**
Aside from standard issues of opening a business in San Francisco, our biggest challenge has been keeping up with the demand for the beer. It's a fun and awesome challenge to have!

# STANDARD DEVIANT BREWING

### What's the atmosphere like?

We promote a laid-back, community feel. Any and all are welcome all the time. It's also a great place for families!

### Are you dog & family friendly?

Yes!

### Do you have food?

We have rotating food trucks.

### What else can you tell us?

The building is not only not level, it's also a parallelogram!

We have a spiral staircase that leads to nothing.

Our bar top is a single 26-foot-long slab of redwood milled from a fallen tree in the Santa Cruz Mountains. ❄

**52**

# TRIPLE VOODOO BREWERY

2245 3rd St., San Francisco, CA 94107
415-598-8811 • triplevoodoo.com

Mon.-Thurs. 4-11 pm; Fri. 3 pm-midnight;
Sat. noon-midnight; Sun. noon-8 pm

**WHEN DID YOU OPEN?**
2010 (2013 at our current location).

**WHAT ARE YOUR MOST POPULAR BEERS?**
Inception Belgian Golden Strong Ale, Anxiety Pils Pilsner, and our IPAS (they rotate constantly).

**WHICH BEERS ARE YOU PROUDEST OF?**
Shadow Boxing Imperial Stout, aged in bourbon barrels. We won our first award (bronze at the Cal. State Fair Commercial Beer Competition) for this beer.

**WHAT'S THE ATMOSPHERE LIKE?**
Triple Voodoo is a premium craft brewery located in the historic Dogpatch neighborhood of San Francisco. We specialize in combining the best qualities of Belgian and West Coast styles of brewing to create unique and interesting beer.

**ARE YOU DOG & FAMILY FRIENDLY?**
Dogs yes; kids no.

**DO YOU HAVE FOOD?**
We serve snacks but do not have a full kitchen (guests are more than welcome to bring in food). We also have food pop-ups from time to time (check the website for schedule).

**WHAT ELSE CAN YOU TELL US?**
We have a constantly rotating list of beer on tap so there is always something new to try.

We are one of the few breweries in SF to offer a wide range of styles. ✽

# HARMONIC BREWING

1050 26th St., San Francisco, CA 94107
415-872-6817 • harmonicbrewing.com

Tues. 4–7 pm; Wed. 3–8 pm; Thurs. 3–11 pm; Fri. 2–11 pm;
Sat. noon–11 pm; Sun. 1–7 pm

**WHEN DID YOU OPEN?**
August 2015.

**WHAT ARE YOUR MOST POPULAR BEERS?**
Harmonic Kolsch, a variety of IPAs, and our signature Rye Old Fashioned Pale.

**WHICH BEERS ARE YOU PROUDEST OF?**
Rye Old Fashioned Pale.

**HAVE ANY OF YOUR BEERS WON AWARDS?**
No. In general, beer is about people and life, not awards.

**WHAT ARE THE BIGGEST CHALLENGES YOUR BREWERY HAS FACED?**
Doing business in San Francisco, one of the nation's most expensive cities, means we have a high cost of doing business. Rent, payroll, taxes, etc. make it difficult to be profitable while still delivering value to our customers. We try to overcome this by sticking to the KISS rule: keep it simple, stupid.

**WHAT'S THE ATMOSPHERE LIKE?**
Industrial-chic setting, but very warm and friendly service. Having an open floor plan, where you can drink a few feet away from our brewhouse and tanks, was a crucial part of our vision. We are a neighborhood gathering place. A running joke is, "Why worry about the born-on date when you can drink right out of the delivery room?"

**DO YOU HAVE FOOD?**
We serve only snacks. Food trucks and pop-ups serve meals three to five times per week, including every Friday and Saturday.

**WHAT ELSE CAN YOU TELL US?**
Cofounders Eddie (bass) and Jon (guitar) play in a quasi-awesome rock band called GRØWLER.

We got the name when Eddie showed up to practice one day, many years ago, with a growler of his homebrew. Our tagline is, "The more beer you drink, the better we sound." Nowadays, we jam on our brewing floor on Sunday nights, and other local brewers, some of our staff, and even some customers join in on the fun.

Staying on the music theme: All kinds of rock and jazz music inspire us. Eddie and our graphic designer friend Andy designed our logo with guitar and amplifier brands in mind. At first glance, you might think we ripped off Gibson, Fender, or Mesa Boogie, but if you compare all those logos to Harmonic's, you'll see that our font is totally unique. ✳

# OLD BUS TAVERN

3193 Mission St., San Francisco, CA 94110
415-843-1938 • oldbustavern.com

Mon.-Thurs. 5:30-10 pm; Fri. 5:30-midnight;
Sat. 10:30 am-midnight; Sun. 10:30 am-9:30 pm

**WHEN DID YOU OPEN?**

July 2015.

**WHAT ARE YOUR MOST POPULAR BEERS?**

Lemon Basil Saison, Starship Rye Lager, and War on Nugs Pale Ale. We brew different pale ales with different hop combinations, and they are consistent top sellers.

**WHICH BEERS ARE YOU PROUDEST OF?**

Deft Funk Dark Sour. This dark, slightly roasty ale was fermented for eight months with a blend of Lactobacillus and three strains of Brettanomyces before aging in French oak soaked in pinot noir. It's tart and funky, with an aroma of sour cherries. I'm most proud of this beer because it was definitely an unusual beer for us. I went way outside my brewing comfort zone and was rewarded with a great tasting beer!

**WHAT ARE THE BIGGEST CHALLENGES YOUR BREWERY HAS FACED?**

As a very small brewery/brew-pub, we are constantly battling our space constraints. In addition to having room for only three fermentation tanks, we share a small walk-in cooler with our kitchen, so it's a challenge to stay organized and make sure we always have cold storage for our packaged beer. However, despite these limitations, we have been able to consistently keep five or six different house beers on our draft list.

Being a brewpub also creates the challenge of maintaining impressive food and bar programs. Brewing beer was the main reason we started Old Bus Tavern, but we also wanted approachable-but-inspired fare from our kitchen and innovative cocktails from our bar. Achieving the right balance of business resources among the brewery, kitchen, and cocktail programs has been an ongoing challenge.

### What's the atmosphere like?

We strive for a thoughtfully designed interior with a casual, relaxed atmosphere. Our guests have complimented our "family vibe," which makes us happy because we are a very tight-knit team and want Old Bus to truly feel like home. We hear repeatedly about our warm and friendly staff, our eclectic playlists, and our vintage VW bus decor that provides a welcoming, retro vibe.

### Are you dog & family friendly?

Family friendly.

### Do you have food?

Whether you're an omnivore or a vegetarian, our aim is to satisfy without weighing you down. Some of our more popular items include cheeseburgers, fish tacos al pastor, and soft pretzel bites with cheddar beer sauce and house-made beer mustard. We're also well known for our chili—whether it's our beef chili, veggie chili, or Frito pie with house-made Fritos.

### What else can you tell us?

With the help of an Indiegogo campaign, we purchased a 1971 VW bus fully dedicated to the business. The Old Bus bus is used for adventures, as well as beer deliveries, festivals, and weddings. It is also available to the community for outdoor parties, events, and catering.

Old Bus Tavern is a music venue! We feature live jazz on Saturday afternoons, as well as Sunday evening performances, and lively rock or DJ shows about once a month on Saturday nights.

Despite warnings about going into business with friends, owner-partners Ben, Jimmy, and John are still best friends and hang out together whenever we have time off (although time off is admittedly rare in this business). ✳

# BARE BOTTLE BREWING CO.

1525 Cortland Ave., San Francisco, CA 94110
415-926-8617 • barebottle.com

Mon.-Thurs. 3-10 pm; Fri. noon-11 pm;
Sat. 11 am-11 pm; Sun. noon-9 pm

**WHEN DID YOU OPEN?**

July 2016.

**WHAT ARE YOUR MOST POPULAR BEERS?**

Galaxy Dust IPA, Muir Woods IPA, Nitro Espresso Macchiato Coffee Milk Stout, Coastal Red Imperial Amber, Scurvy Fighter Pale Ale, Sacred Tart, Doom Bloom Triple IPA, California Cologne Kolsch Style Ale, Yerba Buena Mint Chocolate Porter.

**WHICH BEERS ARE YOU PROUDEST OF?**

Our IPAs are top notch. We combine aromatic hops with peachy Vermont yeast to create our Dust Series IPAs, which are very drinkable and very aromatic. We're extremely proud of the beers where we've made use of local ingredients like SF Sourdough Wheat, Yerba Buena Mint Chocolate Porter, C's

Bees Honey Brown, and Doom Bloom Triple IPA.

**HAVE ANY OF YOUR BEERS WON AWARDS?**

Coastal Red won the Great American Beer Festival Bronze

in 2016; Scurvy Fighter won the bronze at the Cal. State Fair in 2017.

**WHAT ARE THE BIGGEST CHALLENGES YOUR BREWERY HAS FACED?**

We have 300-plus accounts and a huge taproom, so keeping beer in stock is challenging sometimes!

**WHAT'S THE ATMOSPHERE LIKE?**

Our brewery is very laid-back, with an open atmosphere, and it is huge for San Francisco.

**ARE YOU DOG & FAMILY FRIENDLY?**

We are family and dog friendly, which is unusual in San Francisco proper.

**DO YOU HAVE FOOD?**

We have food trucks seven days a week, and we sell fresh pretzels every day.

**WHAT ELSE CAN YOU TELL US?**

We use lots of local ingredients, like yerba buena mint, native SF sourdough lacto cultures, and local honey. ❋

# FERMENT DRINK REPEAT (FDR)

2636 San Bruno Ave., San Francisco, CA 94134
415-825-5657 • fermentdrinkrepeat.com

Tues.-Thurs. 3pm-10 pm;
Fri. & Sat. 3-11 pm; Sun. 2-9 pm

**WHEN DID YOU OPEN?**
June 2016.

**WHAT ARE YOUR MOST POPULAR BEERS?**
El Gringo Cream Ale, Orange Is the New Black (orange-chocolate Belgian stout), Cats in Tracksuits IPA, and Down Cellah New England–style IPA—but we are always changing our beers. We do not have a flagship beer that we always brew. With a seven-barrel system, we have the creative license to brew what we want, when we want.

**WHICH BEERS ARE YOU PROUDEST OF?**
Wit Love Belgian Wit Bier: it won first place in the 2017

Cal. State Fair Commercial Beer Competition!

**WHAT ARE THE BIGGEST CHALLENGES YOUR BREWERY HAS FACED?**

Well, we opened a brewery in one of the most expensive cities in the country, so there's the challenge of making the finances work as a new, small business in San Francisco! But other than that, we have had challenges in getting people to find us because we are located in a somewhat unknown neighborhood on the southern edge of the city. Local residents call the Portola "the best little neighborhood you've never heard of." Because we are south of the intersection of Highways 101 and 280, we are somewhat geographically detached from the city. That said, once people find us, they are won over by the charm and hospitality of our quaint little slice of heaven, and more often than not, they come back to visit us again!

**WHAT'S THE ATMOSPHERE LIKE?**

We set out to create a community space that would be inviting to all who enter—whether they are super beer geeks or people who are brand new to trying craft beers, we want everyone to feel at home. We sought to foster an environment that brings people together, one in which we envisioned people at the bar getting to know each other and, after talking a bit, realizing they actually live only a few doors down from one another here in the Portola. In that vein, besides hearing "the beer is great!," when we hear people comment, "Your taproom feels so warm and welcoming," we believe we've hit our mark.

**ARE YOU DOG & FAMILY FRIENDLY?**

No.

**DO YOU HAVE FOOD?**

We do not serve food. However, we do allow outside food in the taproom.

**WHAT ELSE CAN YOU TELL US?**

We don't have a brew dog ... but we do have a brew cat. Her name is Mama Kitty. We rescued her from the back alley, where we found her with a litter of seven kittens. The kittens were adopted out to our customers (we brought one of the kittens home with us), and Mama Kitty lives in the brewery catching mice—she's a local celebrity.

We were stumped on what to name one of our beers, so we decided to name it something random—thus was born Cats in Tracksuits IPA. Customers would come in and try it based on the name alone. I might also mention that it was one of our top-selling beers. Lure them in with the name ... keep them coming back with the taste! ❈

# LAUGHING MONK BREWING

1439 Egbert Ave., Unit A, San Francisco, CA 94124
415-890-5970 • laughingmonkbrewing.com

Tues.-Fri. 3-10 pm;
Sat. noon-10 pm; Sun. noon-8 pm

**WHEN DID YOU OPEN?**

2016.

**WHAT ARE YOUR MOST POPULAR BEERS?**

Mango Gose and Evening Vespers.

**WHICH BEERS ARE YOU PROUDEST OF?**

Bayview Gold: we support five local community gardens that grow the chamomile for our Belgian-style golden ale.

**HAVE ANY OF YOUR BEERS WON AWARDS?**

Bronze for Session Beer category for Mango Gose at the 2016 Cal. State Fair.

**WHAT ARE THE BIGGEST CHALLENGES YOUR BREWERY HAS FACED?**

Paying rent in San Francisco. We love our city and want to be part of it, but it's pricey.

**WHAT'S THE ATMOSPHERE LIKE?**

Casual, fun, artsy, industrial.

**DO YOU HAVE FOOD?**

We serve snacks and have food trucks several days a week.

**WHAT ELSE CAN YOU TELL US?**

We changed the zoning code so that there could be breweries in our part of the city, which helped our neighbor Seven Stills join us in the Bayview district.

Our founder Andrew Casteel also cofounded Imprint City, an arts nonprofit that supports mural art and education in the Bayview. The nearly dozen murals on our block were all part of Imprint City's annual Bayview Live event happening.

We host a fundraiser for local nonprofits every third Thursday of the month.

We embrace the monastic tradition of service. ✻

# SEVEN STILLS
## BREWERY & DISTILLERY

1439 Egbert Ave., Unit C, San Francisco, CA 94124
415-914-0936 • sevenstillsofsf.com

Tues. & Wed. 4–9 pm; Thurs. 3:30–9 pm; Fri. 3:30–10 pm;
Sat. noon–10 pm; Sun. noon–6 pm

**WHEN DID YOU OPEN?**

July 2016.

**WHAT ARE YOUR MOST POPULAR BEERS?**

Definitely our Hype Can releases, which are usually massively dry-hopped hazy IPAs, and our barrel-aged beers.

**WHICH BEERS ARE YOU PROUDEST OF?**

Eight Pounds per Barrel and our double IPA can releases.

**WHAT ARE THE BIGGEST CHALLENGES YOUR BREWERY HAS FACED?**

Capital to expand.

**WHAT'S THE ATMOSPHERE LIKE?**

Casual, industrial brewery feel, with street art.

**ARE YOU DOG & FAMILY FRIENDLY?**

Yes.

**DO YOU HAVE FOOD?**

Yes.

**WHAT ELSE CAN YOU TELL US?**

In addition to beer, we make whiskey from craft beer. You can visit our brewery and distillery to sample a beer alongside a whiskey made from the same beer. ❊

# ARMSTRONG BREWING CO.

415 Grand Ave., South San Francisco, CA 94080
650-989-8447 • armstrongbrewing.com

Sun.-Tues. 11:30 am-9 pm; Wed. & Thurs. 11:30 am-10 pm;
Fri. & Sat. 11:30 am-11 pm

**WHEN DID YOU OPEN?**
October 2015, but we've been in business since 2012.

**WHAT ARE YOUR MOST POPULAR BEERS?**
415 FOG, South City Brown, Moes Gose, and Nitro Coffee Stout.

**WHICH BEERS ARE YOU PROUDEST OF?**
Durian Pale Ale: it was just something different.

**WHAT ARE THE BIGGEST CHALLENGES YOUR BREWERY HAS FACED?**
We're underground in a historical building, so getting people to find us has been tough.

**WHAT'S THE ATMOSPHERE LIKE?**
Speakeasy that's family friendly.

**ARE YOU DOG & FAMILY FRIENDLY?**
Yes and yes.

**DO YOU HAVE FOOD?**
We do pub fare and barbecue.

**WHAT ELSE CAN YOU TELL US?**
We're known for being innovative, community focused, and focused on beer education. ❋

# South Bay
# and Santa Cruz

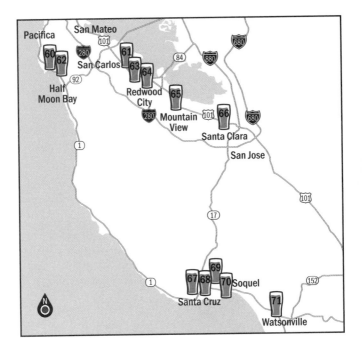

60. Hop Dogma Brewing Co., Half Moon Bay
61. Blue Oak Brewing Co., San Carlos
62. Half Moon Bay Brewing Co., Half Moon Bay
63. Devil's Canyon Brewing Co., San Carlos
64. Freewheel Brewing Co., Redwood City
65. Tied House, Mountain View
66. Taplands, Santa Clara
67. Shanty Shack Brewing, Santa Cruz
68. Uncommon Brewers, Santa Cruz
69. Discretion Brewing, Soquel
70. New Bohemia Brewing Co., Santa Cruz
71. Elkhorn Slough Brewing Co., Watsonville

# HOP DOGMA BREWING CO.

270 Capistrano Rd., Half Moon Bay, CA 94109
650-560-8729 • hopdogma.com

Check website for hours

**WHEN DID YOU OPEN?**

July 2013.

**WHAT ARE YOUR MOST POPULAR BEERS?**

Alpha Dankopotamus IPA, Silly Gimmick New England–style Double IPA.

**WHICH BEERS ARE YOU PROUDEST OF?**

We are proud of our beer in general. We like to think we go the extra mile with all our products, and we are always striving to improve.

**HAVE ANY OF YOUR BEERS WON AWARDS?**

We have won several awards, including honors from the GABF, Cal. State Fair, U.S. Open Beer Championships, Best of Craft Beer Awards, Los Angeles International Beer Competition, and more.

**WHAT ARE THE BIGGEST CHALLENGES YOUR BREWERY HAS FACED?**

Limited supply/production abilities.

**WHAT'S THE ATMOSPHERE LIKE?**

We are located two blocks from the beach and have ocean views from our taproom.

**DO YOU HAVE FOOD?**

We occasionally have food trucks, and patrons are welcome to bring in any food they'd like.

**WHAT ELSE CAN YOU TELL US?**

Hop Dogma operates primarily on a three-barrel system, which is around only 100 gallons at a time. We brew our canned products off-site with trusted partners in the industry. ❋

# BLUE OAK BREWING CO.

821 Cherry Ln., San Carlos, CA 94070
415-283-9676 • blueoakbrewing.com

Thurs. 3:30–8 pm; Fri. 5–11 pm; Sat. 2–11 pm

**WHEN DID YOU OPEN?**
April 2017.

**WHAT ARE YOUR MOST POPULAR BEERS?**
Double IPA, Belgian quad.

**WHICH BEERS ARE YOU PROUDEST OF?**
Belgians, because they are complex and delicious.

**WHAT ARE THE BIGGEST CHALLENGES YOUR BREWERY HAS FACED?**
Too many to name, mostly funding and opening.

**WHAT'S THE ATMOSPHERE LIKE?**
Tiny, homey location in industrial San Carlos.

**DO YOU HAVE FOOD?**
Nope, just bar snacks for now.

**WHAT ELSE CAN YOU TELL US?**
The Blue Oak tree is a species of oak found only in the great state of California.

For thousands of years, the acorns from this tree served as a primary food source for the native tribes and supported a vast ecosystem of local plants and animals.

We wanted a name that honored native Californian roots, and that's when Blue Oak Brewing Company was born! ❉

**62**

# HALF MOON BAY BREWING CO.

390 Capistrano Rd., Half Moon Bay, CA 94019
650-728-BREW (2739) • hmbbrewingco.com

Mon–Thurs. 11:00 am–9 pm; Fri. 11:00 am–10 pm;
Sat. & Sun. 10 am–10 pm

**WHEN DID YOU OPEN?**

2000.

**WHAT ARE YOUR MOST POPULAR BEERS?**

Full Swing IPA, kolsch-style beers, and amber ales.

**WHICH BEERS ARE YOU PROUDEST OF?**

Word on the Street IPA—extremely positive customer response; it has a hoppy goodness and tropical fruit party on your taste buds. Bourbon barrel–aged Damage Inc.—inspired by a brewing attempt in the 1800s to win over the Russian czar, this is the king of stouts, boasting high alcohol and plenty of malt character with huge roasted, chocolate, and burnt malt flavors.

**HAVE ANY OF YOUR BEERS WON AWARDS?**

Winner of a bronze medal at the 2012 World Beer Cup. Winner of a gold medal at the 2015 U.S. Open Beer Championship. Two silver medals at the 2016 Cal. State Fair. Silver medal at the 2015 Cal. State Fair.

**WHAT ARE THE BIGGEST CHALLENGES YOUR BREWERY HAS FACED?**

Keeping up with customer demand for certain beers, especially our barrel-aged series of beers. And keeping our brewing equipment in good working order!

**WHAT'S THE ATMOSPHERE LIKE?**

Fun, casual, family-friendly restaurant resembles a surf shack on the waterfront at Pillar Point Harbor. We have fire pits, a dog-friendly patio, live weekend music, and great food and beer!

**ARE YOU DOG & FAMILY FRIENDLY?**

Yes and yes!

### Do you have food?

We are a brewery and restaurant with a full menu, including a variety of fresh and local seafood, local produce, offering fun bar bites to fish tacos, burgers, and fishermen's stew.

### What else can you tell us?

We were the first legal brewery on the San Mateo County coast since 1873.

We are one of America's top beach bars according to *Travel + Leisure* magazine.

We were the first brewery in California to brew beer with recycled water.

We recycle our grain, giving it to local farmers and making homemade dog bones from it. ✳

**63**

# DEVIL'S CANYON BREWING CO.

935 Washington St., San Carlos, CA 94070
650-592-2739 • devilscanyon.com

Fri: Open at 4 pm

**WHEN DID YOU OPEN?**

October 2001.

**WHAT ARE YOUR MOST POPULAR BEERS?**

Full Boar Scotch Ale, Silicon Blonde Blonde Ale, Deadicated Amber Ale, California Sunshine Rye IPA, Beer Kitty Kolsch, and our barrel aged series.

**WHICH BEERS ARE YOU PROUDEST OF?**

We are most proud of our Full Boar Scotch Ale because it is the beer that put us on the map as a brewery—it's the beer people think about when they think of Devil's Canyon. It brings beer and nonbeer drinkers together. One of the phrases we hear most often from people who try Full Boar is, "Wow! I didn't think I liked dark beers, but this is delicious!"

**HAVE ANY OF YOUR BEERS WON AWARDS?**

Not only has our beer received

several awards, but our brewery has too, including San Carlos Business of the Year and San Mateo County Sustainable Business of the Year. We've received more than 35 craft beer awards as well as the CityVoter People's Choice awards for Best Brewpub and Best Beer Bar.

**WHAT ARE THE BIGGEST CHALLENGES YOUR BREWERY HAS FACED?**

We found a special niche in the brewery market: a family brewery community. We are one of the only breweries around that welcomes kids. We are developing a program to keep kids entertained so families and younger adults can all have a good time at Devil's Canyon.

**WHAT'S THE ATMOSPHERE LIKE?**

We are a family-owned and -operated, certified sustainable business focused on making delicious beer, providing great experiences for our guests, and supporting our community through sustainable and ethical business practices. The brewery hosts private events most of the time, but on Fridays we're open to the public for our weekly family- and kid-friendly Beer Friday, with food trucks, live music, and, of course, craft beer! More than 8,000 visitors and guests come to the brewery every month, and one of the things we hear the most about our space is "Whoa! From outside you would never guess it was so huge and cool looking in here!" and "You built all of this yourselves?!"

### ARE YOU DOG & FAMILY FRIENDLY?
Family friendly.

### DO YOU HAVE FOOD?
Our brewery has a prep kitchen for catered events, and for our public events we work with our local mobile food partner, Off the Grid, to offer all types of cuisines like Hawaiian, Japanese, BBQ, Mexican, Cuban, Italian, and Korean, just to name a few!

### WHAT ELSE CAN YOU TELL US?
We are certified sustainable! Almost everything in the brewery has been reused, reclaimed, or handmade from such materials.

Our Beer Friday events became so popular we needed to add tables and chairs. Instead of buying new tables and chairs, we built them ourselves from the same reclaimed lumber used in our very own taproom.

If you plan to visit our brewery, don't forget to bring your own glass, unless you plan on buying one from us. By encouraging our guests to bring and reuse their own glasses, we cut our water usage immensely. #BYOG

The DCBC Beer Club isn't a bottle-send beer club. It's a social beer club open to anyone who is willing to be on the waiting list for a little while. The Beer Club is limited to 200 people because each member receives their own locker onsite in the Beer Club VIP room. Members also get beer tokens, a special-handled beer mug, and their own dedicated line in the taproom (no waiting for beer!) and members-only events at the brewery. ✽

# FREEWHEEL BREWING CO.

3736 Florence St., Redwood City, CA 94063
650-365-2337 • freewheelbrewing.com

Sun.–Wed. 11:30 am–10 pm;
Thurs.–Sat. 11:30 am–11 pm

**WHEN DID YOU OPEN?**

2013.

**WHAT ARE YOUR MOST POPULAR BEERS?**

FSB (Freewheel Special Bitter)
—this is our traditional cask-
conditioned special bitter. UK
ex-pats always comment that it
reminds them of home. Mind
the Gap IPA is our "English-
American" IPA on keg and
represents our blending of
traditional English and newer
American styles.

**WHICH BEERS ARE YOU PROUDEST OF?**

All our traditional English-
style cask ales are unique and
brewed the right way.

**HAVE ANY OF YOUR BEERS WON AWARDS?**

London Calling, an ordinary
bitter, won the 2013 Cal.
State Fair gold. FSB won the
2013 Cal. State Fair bronze.

**WHAT ARE THE BIGGEST CHALLENGES YOUR BREWERY HAS FACED?**

Introducing cask ale to
NoCal drinkers (an area that

for years was almost exclusively known for hoppy West Coast IPAs).

### What's the atmosphere like?

Laid-back. We pattern ourselves after a more traditional European pub but with a California style. The kind of place you can bring your family. We are very involved in the community and feature local art in the pub, as well as free live music weekly. We also have frequent special events, including a weekly pub quiz, and occasional beer education classes.

### Are you dog & family friendly?

Family friendly.

### Do you have food?

Eclectic pub food.

### What else can you tell us?

We were started by four friends (Malcolm, Larry, Gary, and Pete). Malcolm was the original head brewer and came up with the idea for cask ale after he and Pete (who is English) went on a tour of pubs in the English countryside.

We have two brewers, who both happen to be female. Our head brewer, Alisha Blue, brewed in England before moving back to the States.

We have various passions outside of beer, including music, sports, and art. These passions can be seen in the fabric of Freewheel. ❋

# TIED HOUSE

954 Villa St., Mountain View, CA 94040
650-965-2739 • tiedhouse.com

Mon. 4-10 pm; Tues. & Wed. 11:30-10 pm; Thurs. & Fri. 11:30 am-11:30 pm;
Sat. 10:30 am-10 pm; Sun. 10:30 am-9 pm

**WHEN DID YOU OPEN?**

January 1987.

**WHAT ARE YOUR MOST POPULAR BEERS?**

Our best-selling beer has been and still is Amber.

**WHICH BEERS ARE YOU PROUDEST OF?**

We have made hundreds of different kinds of beers over the past 30-plus years. Our barrel-aged beers, both sour and sweet, are a joy to make and drink. Our Amber beer had been served up till a few years ago at the international space headquarters in Star City, Russia, for decades. Its contribution to better communication between our societies is something we are very proud of.

**HAVE ANY OF YOUR BEERS WON AWARDS?**

GABF, multiple times: Amber, Alpine Gold, Ironwood Dark, New World Wheat, Passion Pale Ale, Raspberry Wheat. Cal. State Fair Commercial Beer Competition: Oatmeal Stout, Alpine Gold, Ironwood Dark. Southern California Sour: Cherry Sour. World Beer Cup: Alpine Gold, Ironwood Dark.

**WHAT ARE THE BIGGEST CHALLENGES YOUR BREWERY HAS FACED?**

Housing costs and traffic congestion that affect our valued skilled craft people in the South Bay Area.

**What's the atmosphere like?**

Large beer hall, beer garden, cafe garden.

**Are you dog & family friendly?**

We are—woof—dog friendly.

**Do you have food?**

We serve great food, all made from scratch with love and care.

**What else can you tell us?**

A (space shuttle) *Challenger* crew member brought a coaster of ours on a trip around the earth. It's on display at the brewpub, along with photos and the astronauts' autographs.

We have served more than 35 million pints of our fresh beer over our bar since we opened, and we have produced more than 62 million pints of beer for local consumption. ✳

**66**

# TAPLANDS

1171 Homestead Rd., #110, Santa Clara, CA 95050
408-709-2990 • taplands.com

Mon.-Wed. 3-10 pm; Thurs. 11 am-10 pm;
Fri. & Sat. 11 am-midnight; Sun. 10 am-10 pm

**WHEN DID YOU OPEN?**
March 2016.

**WHAT ARE YOUR MOST POPULAR BEERS?**
Forty Whacks, a blood orange New England IPA; Sid's Serrano Ale, a smoked serrano pepper pale ale; Pimpin' Porter, a robust chocolate porter; Johnny Mac, a bitter Irish red brewed with rye.

**WHICH BEERS ARE YOU PROUDEST OF?**
Sid's Serrano Ale because it is unique, with heat but still pleases the masses. Whole Lotta Rosey (a blonde ale with vanilla and "bittered" with rose petals instead of hops) because it is an experiment that yielded something truly unique.

**WHAT ARE THE BIGGEST CHALLENGES YOUR BREWERY HAS FACED?**
Space and production volume.

**WHAT'S THE ATMOSPHERE LIKE?**
We have created a very homey neighborhood atmosphere. Our customers tell us it has a vibe that other places lack.

**ARE YOU DOG & FAMILY FRIENDLY?**
Family friendly.

**DO YOU HAVE FOOD?**
Paninis, quesadillas, cheese plates, charcuterie.

**WHAT ELSE CAN YOU TELL US?**
We have a diverse mix of students (we are only one block from Santa Clara University) and neighborhood customers.

We are in the heart of the oldest occupied area of Silicon Valley.

The majority of our customers are able to walk to Taplands. ❄

# SHANTY SHACK BREWING

138 Fern St., Santa Cruz, CA 95060
831-316-0800 • shantyshackbrewing.com

Sun.-Thurs. noon-9 pm;
Fri. & Sat. noon-10 pm

**WHEN DID YOU OPEN?**
December 2016.

**WHAT ARE YOUR MOST POPULAR BEERS?**
So far we have been known for our fruit beers and barrel-aged sours. We also brew great IPAs and switch up which hops we use each time, creating something totally different. Of course, IPAs are the most popular, but our fruited beers are very popular as well!

**WHICH BEERS ARE YOU PROUDEST OF?**
We are proudest of our fresh fruit beers. We've used raspberries, blackberries, olallieberries, and plums. We pick them up from a local farm called Gizdich Ranch.

**WHAT ARE THE BIGGEST CHALLENGES YOUR BREWERY HAS FACED?**
Getting open! Phew. Santa Cruz was tough on us! It took us 20 months of paying rent and working our butts off every day to get open. Nathan and Brandon (the owners and brewers) didn't have any other job during this time. Opening the brewery was their number-one priority and they were on site every day for 15-hour days sometimes.

**WHAT'S THE ATMOSPHERE LIKE?**
We constantly hear people saying they love the vibe at Shanty Shack. With its green walls and rotating local art, it has a relaxing, fun, and easygoing atmosphere. We have a stage and often have live music and rotating food trucks/pop-ups.

**ARE YOU DOG & FAMILY FRIENDLY?**
Our outside patio is dog friendly and the brewery is family friendly.

### DO YOU HAVE FOOD?

We have a kitchen. We serve meat and cheese plates, paninis, and salads, and every Sunday we do "Sun's Out Buns Out Sunday" featuring Brandon's girlfriend's recipes from her hot dog cart: Reuben Dogs, Cubano Dogs, Aloha Dogs, etc. We also have food trucks and pop-ups.

### WHAT ELSE CAN YOU TELL US?

Brandon and Nathan met in a business class in 2012. They started chatting and asked each other why they were taking a business class, and they both had the same answer: "To open a brewery!" They began home-brewing together on Chanticleer Ave. in Santa Cruz and named themselves "Chanti Shack." Once they got a brick-and-mortar building, they decided to change the spelling to Shanty Shack for alliteration purposes.

We have a garden and many plants/herbs on the brewery's premise, and we use cherries,

apricots, blackberries, raspberries, etc., all from Gizdich Ranch in Watsonville.

We have never brewed the same beer twice! We've been open a little over a year and have brewed more than 100 different beers.

We are located right near the train tracks in Santa Cruz. Each time the train goes by with a train full of tourists, we shout "Allllll aboard!" and everyone in the brewery takes a swig of their beer. It's fun! ❋

# UNCOMMON BREWERS

303 Potrero St., Suite 40H, Santa Cruz, CA 95060
831-621-8040 • uncommonbrewers.com

Hours by appointment

**WHEN DID YOU OPEN?**

August 2007.

**WHAT ARE YOUR MOST POPULAR BEERS?**

Siamese Twin Ale, Long Form Tripple, Framboos Blonde Ale.

**WHICH BEERS ARE YOU PROUDEST OF?**

They all have their place and moments. I do love our Baltic Porter and wish that more people were willing to try a dark beer without preconceptions.

**HAVE ANY OF YOUR BEERS WON AWARDS?**

We've taken first in the Cal. State Fair a few times; won awards at the Australian International; and won a bronze at the World Beer Cup for one of our contract recipes.

Competition from big distributors.

**WHAT'S THE ATMOSPHERE LIKE?**

It's fairly industrial

**ARE YOU DOG & FAMILY FRIENDLY?**

We are happy to welcome dogs and families.

**WHAT ELSE CAN YOU TELL US?**

We do not make any of the standard boring beers. Don't expect to see any IPAs on our list; we'll never make one. All our beers are uncommon in one way or another, from lemongrass and kaffir lime leaf in our Siamese Twin Ale to candy cap mushrooms in the Rubidus Red Ale or an entire bacon-cured pork leg in every batch of Bacon Brown Ale. All our beers are uncommon from start to finish.

We were one of the first breweries in the country to do craft cans, starting back in early 2008. ❈

# DISCRETION BREWING

2703 41st Ave., Suite A, Soquel, CA 95073
831-316-0662 • discretionbrewing.com

Daily 11:30 am–9 pm

**WHEN DID YOU OPEN?**
March 2013.

**WHAT ARE YOUR MOST POPULAR BEERS?**
Uncle Dave's Rye IPA and Shimmer Pils.

**WHICH BEERS ARE YOU PROUDEST OF?**
We're honestly proud of all of our beers. We're proving that it's possible to make world-class, award-winning beer using 100 percent organic ingredients.

**WHAT ARE THE BIGGEST CHALLENGES YOUR BREWERY HAS FACED?**
Limited supply of organic ingredients (especially hops)

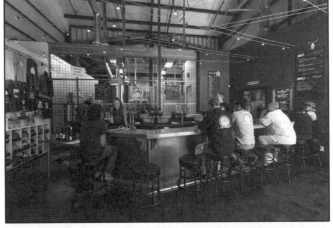

and demand far outpacing production capabilities.

**WHAT'S THE ATMOSPHERE LIKE?**

We have a very laid-back industrial chic vibe. Customers have an open view of the brewery and can enjoy beers in a lovely beer garden where all the plants are edible.

**ARE YOU DOG & FAMILY FRIENDLY?**

We're very family and dog friendly.

**DO YOU HAVE FOOD?**

Discretion has partnered with Chef Santos Majano to run The Kitchen at Discretion. While technically a separate business, ordering is seamless for the customer through a single point of sale. The Kitchen excels at elevated farm-to-table beer-friendly foods. It's some of the best food in Santa Cruz County.

**WHAT ELSE CAN YOU TELL US?**

We're a solar-powered brewery with a solar array that covers roughly 75 percent of our total electrical needs.

Uncle Dave's, our flagship IPA, is named, believe it or not, after Uncle Dave, who lives in the Santa Cruz Mountains and is one of the greatest people on earth to share an IPA with around a campfire.

Even though the head in our logo has an uncanny resemblance to Rob, one of our owners, it's purely coincidental. The graphic artist we hired to create our logo was actually out of the country during the entire design process and had never met or seen Rob! ✳

# NEW BOHEMIA BREWING CO.

1030 41st Ave., Santa Cruz, CA 95062
831-350-0253 • nubobrew.com

Mon.-Thurs. 4-9 pm; Fri. & Sat. 11:30 am-10 pm;
Sun. 11:30 am-9 pm

**WHEN DID YOU OPEN?**
March 2015.

**WHAT ARE YOUR MOST POPULAR BEERS?**
NUBO Pils Pilsner, Highway to Hefe Hefeweizen, Warrior IPA.

**WHICH BEERS ARE YOU PROUDEST OF?**
NUBO Pils Pilsner is an authentic Czech pilsner brewed with German malts and hops and served unfiltered. Monkey Business Dunkelweizen is a traditional Bavarian wheat beer that won the 2015 GABF bronze medal. Cherry Bomb Imperial Stout is a local seasonal favorite brewed with locally sourced cherries and honey; it won the 2016 National Honey Competition for stouts.

**WHAT ARE THE BIGGEST CHALLENGES YOUR BREWERY HAS FACED?**
The success of our beers has

created an ever-growing need for additional brewing capacity and expansion, which can be a challenge to keep up with, but that is a good problem to have.

**WHAT'S THE ATMOSPHERE LIKE?**
Modern but comfortable and inviting. The brewery is a great

place to hang out and soak up
the Santa Cruz vibe.

**ARE YOU DOG & FAMILY FRIENDLY?**
We are family and dog friendly.

**DO YOU HAVE FOOD?**
We serve locally sourced traditional pub food at a reasonable
price, including locally made
Bavarian sausages, cheese and
charcuterie boards, a variety of
German-inspired cheeses, and
house-made pickled vegetables.

**WHAT ELSE CAN YOU TELL US?**
Owner and head brewer Dan
Satterthwaite has the longest
dreadlocks in Santa Cruz.

At any given time, we have
more lagers and hefeweizens on
tap than IPAs. ✺

# ELKHORN SLOUGH BREWING CO.

65 Hangar Way, Unit D, Watsonville, CA 95076
831-288-3152 • elkhornsloughbrew.com

Mon. & Thurs. 4–10 pm; Fri. & Sat. 1–9 pm;
Sun. 1–8 pm

WHEN DID YOU OPEN?

January 2016.

WHAT ARE YOUR MOST POPULAR BEERS?

IPAs and wild ales.

WHICH BEERS ARE YOU PROUDEST OF?

Our wild ales—we use fresh local ingredients and an estate yeast.

HAVE ANY OF YOUR BEERS WON AWARDS?

We've won first place at California Homebrewers.

WHAT ARE THE BIGGEST CHALLENGES YOUR BREWERY HAS FACED?

Meeting demand.

WHAT'S THE ATMOSPHERE LIKE?

We have a family friendly/dog friendly relaxed taproom.

**Do you have food?**

We have food trucks on our open days.

**What else can you tell us?**

We are owned and operated by a local husband/wife team.

We use local yeast and local fruits and hops for beer.

Our brewing philosophy is that by using locally available ingredients, the taste and experience will reflect the beauty of the environment we live in and impart a terroir, or sense of place.

We brew small crafty batches in a three-BBL system at our warehouse in Watsonville.

Yeast is harvested from pressing homegrown apples and allowing them to spontaneously ferment. The wild ales are aged in barrels of all kinds and sometimes combined with other local ingredients to make unique and delicious craft beers. ✻

# Alphabetical List of Breweries

8 Bridges Brewing Co.
86

21st Amendment Brewery
98

Armstrong Brewing Co.
116

Bare Bottle Brewing Co.
110

Bear Republic Brewing Co.
52

Benoit Casper Brewing Co.
66

Black Sands Brewery
100

Blue Oak Brewing Co.
121

The Brewery at Lake Tahoe
32

The Brewing Lair
17

Buffalo Bill's Brewery
84

Channel Brewing
19

Cleophus Quealy Beer Co.
82

DasBrew
88

Devil's Canyon Brewing Co.
124

Discretion Brewing
136

Drake's Brewing Co.
76

Dust Bowl Brewing Co.
24

East Brother Beer Co.
68

Elkhorn Slough Brewing Co.
140

Federation Brewing
78

Ferment Drink Repeat (FDR)
112

Flatland Brewing Co.
18

Fogbelt Brewing Co.
56

Fort Point Beer
94

Freewheel Brewing Co.
126

Gilman Brewing Co.
72

GoatHouse Brewing Co.
36

Half Moon Bay Brewing Co.
120

Harmonic Brewing
106

HenHouse Brewing Co.
62

Heretic Brewing Co.
46

Hop Dogma Brewing Co.
120

Hoppy Brewing Co.
40

June Lake Brewing
20
Laughing Monk Brewing
114
Lost Coast Brewery
10
Mad Fritz
54
Mad River
8
Mare Island Brewing Co.
48
Moonlight Brewing Co.
55
Moonraker Brewing Co.
34
Morgan Territory Brewing
22
New Bohemia Brewing Co.
138
Ocean View Brew Works
70
Old Bus Tavern
108
Port O'Pints
4
Redwood Curtain Brewing
9
Russian River Brewing Co.
58
Sactown Union Brewery
42
Schubros Brewery
80
Seven Stills
Brewery & Distillery
115
Shanty Shack Brewing
132

Sidellis Lake Tahoe
33
Six Rivers Brewery
6
South Gate Brewing Co
26
Standard Deviant Brewing
102
State Room Brewery
92
Taplands
130
Third Street Aleworks
60
Thirsty Bear Organic Brewery
96
Three Forks
Bakery & Brewing Co.
30
Three Mile Brewing Co.
44
Tied House
128
Track 7 Brewing Co.
37
Triple Rock
Brewing & Alehouse
74
Triple Voodoo Brewery
104
Uncommon Brewers
134
Waganupa Brewing
16
Woody's Brewing Co.
14
Yolo Brewing Co.
38

# Cheers

Deirdre Greene lives in the Bay Area, where she drinks a lot of excellent beer. Nigel Quinney lives in San Diego County, where he drinks a lot of equally excellent beer. When they are not drinking beer—and sometimes even when they are—they run Roaring Forties Press, a publishing company that focuses on travel, the arts, popular culture, and contemporary issues.

Deirdre and Nigel have many people to thank for their invaluable support and help during the making of this book. Wesley Palmer deserves all the thanks we can give him for his various and substantial contributions—indeed, Wes should probably be considered a third author for his tireless research, unflagging enthusiasm, inventive ideas, and ability to charm even the grumpiest of brewers! Celia Greene and Ian Decker selflessly spent their holiday visiting breweries on our behalf.

Our design and production team were outstanding. Kim Rusch came up with the perfect covers. Karen Weldon laid out the book with wonderful flair and professionalism; we don't know what we do without her. Kaileen Smith produced precise but unfussy maps—no small achievement! And Carla Castillo helped catch a small army of pesky typos.

Researching and producing a book like this takes a lot of time. Pleased don't get us wrong: we're not complaining about that, especially because a lot of that time was in breweries! (As Wes has often remarked, researching the craft beer industry is surely one of the best jobs around.) But we're grateful to our families, who also didn't complain about the time we spent putting this book together. Deirdre would like to thank John, Celia, Sophie, and Phoebe. Nigel owes a very big thanks to Kim, Juliet, and Beckett.

This book could not, of course, have been produced without the help of the people it spotlights: the brewers, brewery owners, brewery staff, and everyone else who make California craft brewing the toast of this beer-loving nation. We are indebted to them for their readiness to answer our questions and unearth all sorts of photos and artwork. As this book makes clear, craft brewing demands buckets of skill, energy, and love, and we are very grateful that, despite all the other demands on their time, the brewers featured in this book were prepared to share their experiences, thoughts, and stories with us. ✳

# Notes

# Notes

# Notes

# Notes

# Notes

# Notes

# Notes

# Notes